Dannii

My Story

Dannii

My Story

Dannii Minogue

**SIMON &
SCHUSTER**

London · New York · Sydney · Toronto

A CBS COMPANY

First published in Great Britain in 2010 by Simon & Schuster UK Ltd
A CBS COMPANY

Copyright © 2010 by KDB Artists Pty. Ltd.

1 3 5 7 9 10 8 6 4 2

Simon & Schuster UK Ltd
1st Floor
222 Gray's Inn Road
London
WC1X 8HB

www.simonandschuster.co.uk

Simon & Schuster Australia
Sydney

A CIP catalogue copy for this book is available
from the British Library.

ISBN: 978-0-85720-052-5 (Hardback)
ISBN: 978-0-85720-053-2 (Trade paperback)

Typeset by M Rules
Printed in the UK by CPI Mackays, Chatham ME5 8TD

Dannii

My Story

For my family who have always been there
with love and open arms

For Kris and Ethan Edward who are my world

In loving memory of my dear friend Laura

Contents

This Isn't How It Was Supposed to Be

Having a baby: joyful, a quiet celebration with family. An intimate and magical moment of discovery shared with your partner. Hmmm . . . I wish!

Tuesday, 24 November 2009

The car is stuck in rainy London traffic and, as usual, I'm running on what some of my closer friends would call 'Minogue Time', which basically means I'm late. For most of the afternoon, I'd been hurtling around Somerset House on ice skates, filming a segment for *The X Factor* with one of my contestants, Stacey Solomon. It was all good fun, but now I'm tired, and I'm wilting into the soft leather back seat of a very slow moving Jaguar.

My friends, Sam and George, are due to arrive at my apartment in Battersea at any minute for supper and I'm not even close to home. What's worse is that I've recklessly opted to make my much-lauded veggie lasagne tonight, which, as the cooks among you know, takes some time to prepare and then an hour or so on top of that to bake, so I'll almost certainly have to rustle up a hearty salad as soon as I get in to keep us going in the meantime.

Damn! My BlackBerry is ringing again and it's a work call. I feel too tired to talk. I just want to get home and chop vegetables.

'Hello!'

At least the car is moving now.

'Hi, D.'

It's Nathan, who works for my management, and he's chuckling. 'You're gonna laugh at this,' he says, cautiously.

Something tells me I won't.

'Simon from our PR company has just called to say that a national newspaper is claiming that you're three months pregnant and that you went for a scan at the weekend. They're running it front page tomorrow and want us to comment – isn't that ridiculous?'

I don't answer. I'm numb and I feel slightly faint.

'Obviously, need to confirm with you that it's a load of rubbish before I get back to them,' Nathan says.

I still don't answer and now I can hear my own breath.

'D?'

'Er . . . can I call you when I'm out of the car?' I ask him flatly.

'Oh!'

When I usher Sam and George into my apartment, minutes after I get in myself, I settle them in the lounge and tell them I have to make a quick business call before I start dinner.

'Guys, pour yourselves a glass of wine,' I say. 'I won't have one. No, it's fine – really. I'm too tired. I need to be fresh for work tomorrow. I'll just pop some music on . . . Sorry about this . . . Won't be long.'

I wonder if I got away with that. Do they think it's odd I'm not having a glass of wine with them?

Now quite flustered, I dash into my bedroom, which is next to the lounge, and call Nathan and tell him the truth. He tries to calm me down, then puts me on to Simon, my publicist, who informs me that the newspaper is going to print with the pregnancy story. Front cover. In thirty minutes. It's literally sitting on the press waiting for the editor to give the go-ahead to run it.

'Simon,' I whisper urgently. 'You've got to help me. How can we stop them running this story? Yes, I'm pregnant, but only about six weeks. Kris knows, of course, but we haven't even told our parents yet. I want to tell my mum and dad face to face when I go back to Australia, not like this, not splashed across the papers . . . I can't breathe, hang on a sec . . .'

My face feels flushed and my palms are sweating and shaking – so much that I almost drop the phone. I pop my head around the bedroom door.

'Sorry, guys. Won't be long,' I call out to Sam and George. 'I'm doing a lasagne for dinner. Nice?'

Back to the call.

'Seriously, is there a way we can stop this?'

It turns out that the only way we can stop it is by admitting to the newspaper that I am, in fact, pregnant, but just six weeks. Simon informs me that it's an infringement of a woman's rights for any media to make a pregnancy public knowledge before the three-month scan. If the newspaper knows for sure I'm only six weeks pregnant, then they can't print the story.

'But I have to call Kris and ask him if it's OK first,' I say, now brimming over with tears. 'I'll try to get hold of him now and get back to you.'

'We have to do it soon, Dannii, or they'll run the story anyway,' Simon says, solemnly. 'Call me straight back.'

I try calling Kris, but it's 5:30a.m. in Australia and his phone is off. I text him and then try calling him again but still there's no answer. The clock is ticking. My blood is running hot and cold. What do I do?

I stick my head out of the bedroom again.

'Won't be long now, boys. Help yourselves to more wine. Chat among yourselves and all that!'

Right. I'm going to have to make this decision all on my own, aren't I? I've already had to tell my management and my PR company that I'm pregnant before I was ready to; now I'm going to have to tell a national newspaper too, just in time to stop the whole world from finding out – even before Kris and I have had a chance to tell our families and friends the happy news, and while cooking a veggie lasagne. This isn't how it was supposed to be.

Dannii

My Story

Chapter 1

Gumboots and Tutus

M y life hasn't always been quite this convoluted, of course. It's often at moments like this, when I feel slightly out of control or a little bit misplaced, that I try to remember a simpler and more tranquil past: times spent at home in our back garden in Wantirna, wearing a big toothy smile, head to toe in mud and ecstatic with my latest catch of frogs or blue-tongued lizards, with my brother, Brendan.

What? Dannii Minogue? Covered in mud and grappling with a big, fat scaly lizard? Can you imagine? Most of my friends now can't imagine, but it's true. It's where it all began.

We lived in what my dad called a 'battler's area', which was a suburb of Melbourne called Scoresby. It was full of struggling young families with new mortgages and very little money. There were no roads, no footpaths and, believe it or not, no sewage. Dad worked as an accountant at a place called Mackay's in Moorabbin, while Mum had a part-time job dishing out cups of tea at the local hospital. In comparison to now it was pretty much a 'no frills' way of life. We lived in Scoresby until I was about three.

My brother, sister and I had all come into the world while Mum and Dad were living at their previous house in South Oakleigh, Melbourne. I was born in Bethlehem – that's the hospital, not the holy city – on 20 October 1971: Danielle Jane Minogue, the third and last child of Ron and Carol Minogue. Apparently, I was very late – about two and a half weeks – and Mum always says that nothing much has changed since then.

My earliest memories are mostly of playing with my brother, Brendan; I guess because we were closest in age – only seventeen months apart. Brendan was the one I could attempt to keep up with because my sister, Kylie, who was a whopping three years older than me and therefore much more grown-up, would be off playing with the bigger girls and doing her own thing. The consequence of this was, of course, that I played the games and did all the stuff that my big brother wanted to play and do, so I became a complete and utter bloody tomboy.

To be honest, I remember having only one doll that I'd pestered Mum and Dad for at Christmastime. She was a Baby Alive doll: you could feed her, and she would pee and cry and do all the things real babies do. Apart from that I wasn't into girlie stuff and was just as content playing with the toy trucks and cars that Brendan left lying around. I did have a few homemade knitted teddies and a toy Snoopy dog, which I loved and still have now.

When Brendan was feeling mischievous and was well out of Mum's vigilant sightline, he'd kidnap Snoopy and peg him to the washing line by his ears so I couldn't reach him. He'd then test my mettle by drenching poor Snoopy with the garden hose, which distressed me no end, and I'd be screaming and beside myself until I got him back safely in my arms. I can't remember how many times my brother subjected Snoopy – or any of my other poor down-at-heel knitted teddies – to this terrible torture, but it's a very vivid memory.

Kylie and her cooler, older girlfriends would often play a game called elastics, which some people called French skipping. This involved two girls standing a couple of metres apart with a bit of elastic tied in one big circular loop around their ankles. Then a third girl in the middle had to do a sequence of jumps in, on and around the stretched elastic. The elastic got hiked upwards as the game progressed: first to the knees, then bums, waists and up around the two girls' necks, so the one in the middle had to jump higher and higher until it became impossible. It was brilliant, uncomplicated fun and a cheap game to get together. I often wonder why you don't see girls playing it these days. Anyway, *sometimes*, and only sometimes, I'd be allowed to have a go at elastics with Kylie and her friends. For the most part, though, it was a game for the bigger girls, so, more often than not, I'd end up back in the mud with Brendan.

I didn't care. I loved being outside more than anything, and my brother and I were happiest when we were covered in dirt or drenched with water from the garden sprinkler. We also loved to find and collect frogs and lizards, particularly blue-tongued lizards, often spotted in the suburban garden areas around Melbourne. These lizards are big, thick and fat – about the size of a hot dog – and great fun to catch.

I was such a tomboy, in fact, that even my name, Danielle, started to annoy the hell out of me as I got a bit older. There was a very famous Aussie-rules football star and journalist called Dan Minogue, who was no relation to us, but we'd often hear people asking Dad: 'So are you related to Dan Minogue, the footy player, then?' I couldn't for the life of me understand why my parents hadn't named *me* Dan or Danny. To my mind, you didn't have to have a girl's name or a boy's name – they were all just names.

'I want to be called Danny!' I'd tell anyone who'd listen.

Our house in Deauville Court, Wantirna, is the first house I really remember – we moved there in 1974 and stayed for about five years. It's completely suburban now, but then beautiful apple orchards sur-rounded us. I remember feeling very free there, and safe. The house was on a corner looking into a court and there were always loads of other kids to play with, tearing around and riding our bikes in the street all day until our mums came out and called us for tea – so very differ-ent to today.

There was much more of a community vibe then. There had to be – nobody could afford nannies or babysitters or anything like that. You relied on your extended family and the people who lived around you. Someone might pop a head around your back door and yell, 'I need you to mind my kids for an hour and then I'll be back.' And the next week she'd do the same for you. You lived very much within the community of your particular street, and all the people on it were a big part of your world. In fact, with hindsight, it was a lot like Ramsey Street in *Neighbours*.

Our next-door neighbours at that time were Frank and Dawn, who were a mixed race South African couple – quite unusual for Melbourne in those days – and they were kind and gracious friends. They were fabulous cooks and loved their food. They were both rather large; our family seemed tiny in comparison. Sometimes Dawn would pop by with delicious and exotic spicy foods for us to try. Once I picked and ate what I thought was a red capsicum from their garden, only to have my whole mouth ablaze moments later. I'd bitten into a hot chilli pepper, and it sent me running in to Mum, screaming blue murder.

Another time I remember a huge commotion and dreadful shouting coming from Frank and Dawn's house – screaming like you couldn't imagine. Dad was convinced they were trying to kill one another but, as it turned out, they'd just been trying to wallpaper a very small toilet together, which, Dad said, barely one of them could fit into, let alone both of them.

We still weren't all that well off then but we never wanted for anything – even a swimming pool wasn't out of the question. Dad set up an above-ground pool in our back garden; we adored it, and played and played in it for hours under the scorching sun. There would always be at least ten kids from the neighbourhood in that pool at any given time. Dad says it was probably full of snot, pee and God knows what, and you could probably walk Jesus-like across the water, but we didn't mind. We all jumped in and out of it and nobody ever got sick. Dad would just chuck some chlorine in it every few days. We loved it!

One memorable Christmas, I got my very first bicycle, and I was terribly excited. It wasn't exactly a new bike – in fact, it was my brother's old one that Dad had lovingly refurbished and repainted. We had a grand ceremonial unveiling in Dad's garage, and I couldn't have been happier. I didn't know, or even care, that it wasn't brand new. As far as I was concerned, it was a bike, and it had streamers, which Dad had attached to the handlebars, and training wheels and a basket with a flower on it. I was over the moon.

Of course, Brendan saw my pretty 'new' bike as an opportunity for him to test my skills as a daredevil stuntwoman – something he was very fond of doing when we were growing up. One bright afternoon, we were both at the top of a steep hill when Brendan said, 'Hey, Danielle! Let's see how fast you can go down.' That's what boys do, right? They dare one another to do dangerous stuff. With me often being the only one around, and being a bit of a tomboy, all the dangerous stuff seemed to come my way. That particular day I found myself hurtling down the hill, unable to stop, not knowing how to control the bike or use the brakes, or anything. At some point during this terrifying ride, the pedal of my new bike came off, and to this day I have a very visible scar on my leg where the exposed metal of the broken pedal jammed into my skin.

This was only one of the many times Brendan encouraged me to stare death in the face as a child. As an adult I've got my motorbike licence, jumped out of planes and swum with sharks – and I've loved the experiences. I truly believe that if it hadn't been for my brother and his perilous dares, I would almost certainly not have had the strong lust for adventure that I have.

As a little girl, I loved hearing the story about how Mum and Dad met at a barn dance at a place called The Powerhouse in 1964, when Mum was a ballerina. There she was, blonde and beautiful in a gorgeous black cowl-neck dress, cut low at the back, while Dad was on the other side of the room wearing stovepipe jeans and too much California poppy oil in his hair. He was not, however, wearing his customary Clark Kent-style glasses, which he always took off to impress the girls. Dad had spotted Mum earlier in the evening and thought, 'That's the girl for me.' He decided to ask her out as soon as he got to dance with her. By the time they were finally partnered up for a do-se-do, he couldn't tell, without his glasses, if she was the girl he was dancing with. He went ahead and asked her out anyway; as it turned out, it was indeed Mum. They got married in October 1965.

Both of them were always very loving and fair in the way they brought us up. Mum was definitely the one with the softer touch, while Dad enforced the rules, which I think was the norm for most of the families I knew back then. Mum and Dad have always been quite traditional in their marriage: Dad runs the house and finances, and Mum runs everything else.

Dad gave us a small amount of pocket money each week, which was just enough to buy some sweets. I didn't like sweets much, so while Brendan and Kylie would dash to the shops for a Golden Gaytime (I kid you not) or a Drumstick, which were both types of ice cream, my favourite thing to buy from the newsagents was swap cards, which had pictures of animals or football players or cars on them. Kids would collect, swap and attach them to the spokes of their bikes to make an exciting clackety-clack sound as they zoomed around.

I adored anything to do with fashion and dressing up. When I was still little, with white-blonde hair, my absolute favourite thing was to team a tutu and gumboots (or wellingtons, as the Brits call them) as one magnificent outfit. The tutu, I reckon, came from a fixation I had with pictures of my mother as a ballerina when she was younger, and wanting to emulate her poise and femininity. Perhaps the gumboots, which were bright yellow and had 'stop' and 'go' written on either foot, were there to reaffirm my status as a little tomboy . . . as Danny.

Our grandparents were a very big and important part of our young lives. So much of what I learned from them has helped fashion the woman I am today. They were always around when we were kids, and would sometimes babysit us so Mum and Dad could have a bit of well deserved time off. My dad's mum has always been 'Nana', and her husband, my step-grandfather, we call 'Grand-pop' because he's American. Nana always had beautiful cutlery and serving dishes, and she would teach Kylie, Brendan and me how to lay the table and how to make and serve tea in a proper teapot. After we'd eaten at Nana's, the three of us kids would be expected to help clean up, as there weren't dishwashers then. One of us would wash up, one would dry and the other would put away, and we'd take each chore in turn whenever we were there. Nana showed us how to do these little tasks correctly. That's something that I really want to do with my kids too – teach them all those good old-fashioned ways of doing things.

We know my mum's mother as 'Nain' and her dad was 'Taid' as they are Welsh. Nain, who is now ninety and still going strong, migrated to Australia from a place called Maesteg in South Wales with Taid and their four children in 1955 – Mum would have been about ten. The journey took a gruelling six weeks, most of which Nain says she spent sick in bed. The ship they travelled on was named *The New Australia*; ironically, it was on its final voyage before being sold to Japan for scrap. In those days, you had to be nominated by a relative to come and live in Australia, and Nain had an aunt who lived on a sugar cane farm near Townsville, Queensland, so that's where they settled. Nain instantly fell in love with the place, and with seeing the sun every day. Once settled in the tropics, she and Taid added two more kids to their brood.

Whenever we were with Nain, she was either sewing or cooking. We'd be in the kitchen, and Nain would whip up scones, or cookies, or cakes. She'd wield a rolling pin, and there would be clouds of white flour filling the kitchen and dusting the bench. She used to make clothes for us all, as did Mum, so there was always a Singer or a Janome sewing machine around, and the house would quite regularly be covered in all types of fabrics and cottons, plus beads, buttons and sequins and pins all over the floor. Nain had brought up six children with very little money, so rather than buying new clothes when they were needed, she had to make them, and then I guess she just carried on making them for her grandkids.

I was completely fascinated with clothes and fashion from a very young age. While I wasn't particularly eager to use the sewing machine myself, I was totally spellbound by all the fabrics and the patterns and what we could make with them, and, as I got older, how we might change the pattern to make something completely unique – something only I would wear. Kylie was always a whizz on the sewing machine, and loved making things herself, but I wanted to create a design in my head and then get someone else to do the hard work for me. To tell you the truth, it's pretty much the same now: I'm really good at coming up with unique ideas and designs for clothes, but I can't draw them very well, and I don't have the skills to sew and make them myself either. From my very first fashion statement with the gumboots and tutu, however, I was hooked.

My memories of the house in Deauville Court, Wantirna, are incredibly happy on the whole. We weren't wealthy, no, but we were loved and looked after, and I learned so much from my grandmas, and from my parents too. I think many kids did then. They learned how to cook and how to make things and mend things, and I loved that about being a kid. I wish the world were a bit more like that now.

Chapter 2

That's Not My Canary

Mum and Dad moved from house to house every few years after we were born, renovating as they went. Each house they bought was a bit of a dump at first, but then Mum and Dad would gradually spruce it up and sell it on, each time moving to a nicer area and into a bigger house that needed even more TLC. Dad would always say, 'Buy the worst house in the best street and then do it up!'

Today, I can appreciate what they were doing, but as kids, of course, we didn't understand this strange and, as we saw it, daft philosophy. We got our houses all pretty and just the way we wanted them, then we'd move to yet another dump and live in an even bigger mess. 'What's the point of that?' we'd all demand to know, petulantly.

Anyway, we moved to a new place in St John's Avenue in Camberwell, Melbourne in 1979, when I was around seven or eight. The house had the most hideous, garish tiles and patterned lino throughout, and, like a lot of houses in the seventies, bright flocked wallpaper on every single wall. The whole place needed a lot of work – in fact, at one point half the floor was missing – but for the first time I had my own bedroom, which was tremendously exciting.

In the house in Wantirna, I'd had to share a room with big sister Kylie. Although we usually got on pretty well, like all siblings we did sometimes get into fights. It was never anything major, but she was someone I very much looked up to, so I'd always ask to borrow things, or want to know exactly what she was doing every minute of the day. After one quarrel, when I was six or seven, I remember her sticking a line of thick black tape right down the middle of the room – a dark, forbidding border dividing the territories.

'That's your side,' Kylie informed me firmly, 'and this is my side!'

I eagerly nodded in agreement, looking towards the door, which was on my side of the room.

I guess it must have been hard for her being the older girl and having a little sister hanging around all the time. We were both over-joyed when we each finally had our own space.

The house in St John's Avenue, Camberwell, had another big plus to it, which we all adored, and that was the rumpus room. This fun-packed area was right at the back of the house, past the lounge and all the bed-rooms, and was the thoroughfare to the back garden. The rumpus room was all things to all people. It had a pool table that turned into a ping-pong table, which was used non-stop, especially by Brendan and all his mates; a piano, which Kylie was learning to play; and, right in the corner, a birdcage where my beloved canary, Bluey, lived.

This lovely little bird would sing beautifully for me every morning, and I'd feed him little bits of apple, or put cuttlefish in his cage for him to peck at, and sometimes I'd let him out to fly around the room – always making sure the back door was tightly shut, of course. I absolutely loved him and I promised Mum faithfully when I got him that I'd look after him myself.

'Don't worry, Mum,' I said. 'I'll clean out his cage and feed him. I'll be the one looking after him.'

But, of course, half the time Mum would end up doing it herself, as I'd be off playing somewhere and forget all about it.

The sun-filled rumpus room was without a doubt where all the action was. Kylie would be hammering away at her piano and my canary would be singing, while Brendan and his mates would endeavour to drown them out by turning up their KISS or AC/DC records on the stereo while they were playing pool. The house was a noisy and happy if slightly insane place to be, and I have exceptionally fond memories of it.

For our first holidays when I was little, we'd go to Phillip Island, which is a popular family holiday destination about 140 kilometres from Melbourne. Back then, holidays smelled of fish and chips, vinegar, ice cream, the beach and suntan lotion, and they were magical. We would stay in a caravan by the water, and we'd spend most of the time running around in the sand or sun-baking in our bathers.

On one scorching Australian summer day, Dad fell fast asleep in the sun, and the three of us kids drew a smiley face on his stomach in thick sunblock. He was there for ages while we played. When he finally woke up, he was bright red from head to foot except for two white eyes and a grinning mouth across his belly. These days, with all the things we now know about the dangers of getting sunburned, you'd never leave someone asleep cooking on the beach for that long. It seems horrific now, but at the time we all thought it was hilarious – except Dad, of course.

The whole family would gather on a picnic blanket and watch Phillip Island's famous fairy penguins come up out of the water each evening just as the sun was going down. These tiny penguins would, as a rule, return to their colonies in groups at this time to feed their chicks, and we'd all be enchanted, letting our eyes adjust to the dim light of dusk as we watched their little parade. There's a whole viewing area there these days, with concrete stands and lights and scores of people coming to watch the fairy penguins every night, but I remember when it was just me, Kylie and Brendan with Mum and Dad, watching from a little plaid blanket by the water.

As we got older and outgrew the caravan, we'd drive up to Surfers Paradise in Queensland, which was something like a twenty-hour drive in those days. We loved it there as teenagers: a beach resort chock-a-block with fast-food joints and theme parks galore – what wasn't to love? Mum and Dad hated it, and I guess it's not the first place I'd pick for a vacation these days either.

Back at home in Camberwell, Mum and Dad loved to entertain, and had lots of dinner parties. They didn't have much money to go out, and Mum says there weren't all that many places to go then even if they had, so their friends would come over for a regular get-together at the house. Mum would serve up sliced salami with cubed cheese and cocktail onions on sticks, and follow it with a spaghetti bolognese or the occasional fondue. For an added touch of class, there were after-dinner mints at the end of the meal, and we kids would always hope to find some left in the box the next morning.

Once again, on those nights, the rumpus room would come into its own. We'd all end up playing records there and dancing around like mad after dinner. Mum and Dad always had great taste in music. The two albums I remember over the years were Stevie Wonder's *Songs In The Key of Life* and Roberta Flack's *Killing Me Softly*; I still love both artists and albums today.

I was becoming as wildly obsessed with music as I was with fashion. When the movie *Grease* came out, a year or so before we moved to Camberwell, I remember Kylie and I going completely nuts over Olivia Newton-John and the movie's soundtrack. We gyrated on top of our imaginary cars in the lounge and did the dance routine to 'Greased Lightning' over and over again. Kylie wanted to be Sandy, but I always secretly wanted to be Rizzo, the bad girl.

The other group I was completely obsessed with back then was ABBA. I was under the spell not only of the music, but also of Agnetha and Frida's fabulous costumes: silver platform boots and blue pantaloons, corresponding satin catsuits and the obligatory understated glittery cape. They were super-successful in Australia, and there had been something akin to Beatlemania when they came over for a concert tour in 1977.

In Camberwell, we lived next door to a bloke called Harry, who had always lived with his mother. While my mum and dad were making our house in St John's Avenue more and more lovely as time went on, Harry and Mrs Jenkins lived in very poor circumstances. The house was quite dishevelled, and they never had anything electrical. In fact, all they had to heat the house with was an old-fashioned brickette heater that used pressed coal and turned all their walls dark; they never put it on until after six o'clock even when it was very cold.

Harry was a slightly odd chap. A war veteran who proudly went to the Anzac parade in all his medals, he lacked confidence after years of very serious alcoholism, and therefore couldn't work. By the time we knew him, though, he was completely on the wagon. Harry often spent his days wandering around Camberwell with his head down, eyes to the ground, hoping to find coins or, if his luck was in, the odd note along the pavement.

Mum used to drive Mrs Jenkins to the doctor when she needed to go, and I remember Mum and Dad once taking them both for a big day out at the races. In turn, Harry would always keep an eye out for us kids, and I recall having a particularly special friendship and connection with him. Harry would teach me all sorts of useful stuff that he'd learned in wartime that I'd never have got from school: how to keep warm if you had no heat by lining things with newspaper and, believe it or not, how to cook and eat a lobster.

After finding some money on the street one day, Harry headed straight to the food market – not to buy meat and three veg but a fresh, live lobster. Of course, this was a luxury item and not something he'd be able to get his hands on very often, but Harry took great delight in sharing his lobster with me, and he taught me exactly how to prepare and enjoy it at its best.

'Never smother it with sauce and stuff,' he said. 'Just squeeze some fresh lemon on it and add some salt and pepper to bring out the flavour. Enjoy it as it is.'

Then he taught me to crack it and eat it properly, and exactly where all the best bits of meat were hidden. I've sometimes stopped and smiled when I've found myself in magnificent restaurants around the world, from Hôtel Costes in Paris to Claridge's in London. I might be much more worldly these days, but it's ironic to think that I can order a lobster with confidence, and know exactly what I'm doing with it, because of the nice old war veteran who lived next door to us all those years ago.

*

My school, Camberwell Primary, was right around the corner from the house. It was a gorgeous old red-brick building with old-fashioned wooden desks and chairs, and it stood in a charming little playground. In the blazing heat of summer the teachers would open all the windows, and I'd lie slumped over my desk, trying to concentrate, while listening to the high chirruping choir of cicadas in the trees outside the classroom.

My best friend there was Jacqui, a wonderful girl with long strawberry-blonde hair, freckles and cute round glasses. Jacqui was very studious – much more so than I was; in fact, she was a complete bookworm, and I really looked up to her. We both regularly got good grades, but I remember that we would laugh and laugh so much in class that we often had to be separated to save the sanity of the teacher. I was never one to have tons and tons of friends. Jacqui and I spent all our time together and never cared whether or not we were in the cool group or the not-so-cool group – it was just the two of us.

There was, I recall, one boy at Camberwell Primary who made it clear to everyone that he didn't like me at all – Fat Billy. I remember Fat Billy very clearly because he seemed to have a twisted fascination with me. He picked on me and teased me relentlessly in an attempt to get my attention, and I hated him. However, this was where having an older brother came in handy. If things got sticky, I would call on Brendan and his mate Frenchy to come and keep Billy in line. Still, whenever he got the opportunity, Fat Billy made my life hell, tripping me up in the playground, throwing things at me and generally being a bully. To be honest, I can't imagine what became of him. He was always so busy getting involved in other people's business and trying to ruin things for them that he was never particularly proactive in his own affairs, and never achieved good grades or had many real friends.

On 16 February 1983, a blistering hot, dry day towards the end of my time at Camberwell Primary, we tore out of the classrooms to look at the skies, which had turned an eerie black. It looked just like one of those 'end of the world' movies, and for a while we had absolutely no idea what it was. The ominous cloud turned out to be ash that had risen in the heat from the horrific bushfires raging out of control in the Dandenong Ranges that day. The whole of Melbourne was literally surrounded by fire. As we stood transfixed in the playground, a huge, dark blanket covered the entire city. This terrible event became known as Ash Wednesday and saw the worst bushfires in Australian history until the fires of 2009. More than seventy people died, as well as a countless number of livestock and native animals, and thousands of people lost their homes. Seeing the black skies above our school that day is something I'll never forget.

One afternoon I came home from school and dashed straight to the rumpus room to see my beloved Bluey. It didn't take me long to figure out that something wasn't quite right, and eventually I went to find and confront Mum on the matter.

'Mum, that's not my canary,' I said, hands on hips. 'I don't know who that is, but it's definitely not my canary.'

Then Mum 'fessed up. She'd been cleaning out Bluey's cage and he'd somehow got out while the back door was open and flown away. I was horrified. Mum assured me that she had looked and looked but was unable to find him, and, in the end, had conceded defeat. She'd been so afraid of telling me the horrendous truth about my fugitive bird, knowing I'd be completely broken-hearted, that she'd gone straight to the pet shop and bought another yellow canary that she thought looked similar enough for me not to notice. Of course, there was no fooling me, and I was inconsolable, leaving Mum feeling awful. No, I didn't want the new canary, however pretty he was, I wanted Bluey and that was that.

Suddenly, amid my seemingly interminable anguish, there was a knock at the front door. When we opened it, there stood my friend, Harry, the old soldier from next door, and nestled delicately in his cupped hands was Bluey. Harry had spotted him in the tree in his garden during Mum's desperate search earlier in the afternoon but hadn't been able to catch him. Eventually, though, Harry, just like the hero I knew he was, had rescued Bluey, knowing how much I loved him, and was now delivering him safely back to me. I was overjoyed.

'That's my canary!' I smiled.

Thanks, Harry.

Chapter 3

Just Like Olivia

I wanted to perform before I really knew what being a performer meant. I didn't know, or understand, that it was a profession or a job that you could actually get paid for. All I knew was that people who sang and danced were on TV and in the movies, all looking like they were having a great time, and I wanted to do it too.

As we got a bit older, Brendan, Kylie and I were each allowed to participate in one weekly after-school activity that Mum and Dad would pay for and ferry us back and forth to. Kylie loved her piano lessons. I'd also had a shot at the piano but wasn't too fussed about continuing. I thought that I'd like to try singing, but I wasn't sure it was quite enough.

'I want to learn how to sing *and* dance,' I announced to Mum. 'Like Olivia Newton-John does in *Grease*. She sings *and* she dances. I want to be just like Olivia.'

Mum and Dad didn't know where to start, not having been brought up in performing or show-business families, so Dad opened the *Yellow Pages* and began searching for a talent school, or club, that was both close by and reputable, where I might be able to give my burgeoning theatrical itch a bit of a scratch.

'What about this place?' Dad suggested.

He was pointing at the biggest ad in the section, which was for the Johnny Young Talent School – that was a name we all knew! Much like *The X Factor* is in the UK today, *Young Talent Time* was a hugely popular prime-time Saturday-night TV show in Australia, and had been since before I was born. We never missed it in our house. It was a bit like *The Mickey Mouse Club* in America, with a regular core team of youngsters performing glitzy, fun musical numbers and pop hits of the day, plus a junior talent contest each week. Johnny Young was the well-known, enigmatic creator and presenter of the programme; he'd been a pop star in Australia in the sixties. His warm demeanour, flashy clothes and wonderfully corny delivery had made him and the programme a massive hit with both old and young, and some of the team members from the TV show had come from his talent school. Yes, this was definitely the place for me!

Mum wasn't especially keen on me singing and dancing, as she'd been a dancer when she was young and knew how tough it could be, but Dad phoned the school and said that he would take me if I really wanted to go, so it was settled. At the grand old age of seven, I was going to the Johnny Young Talent School to learn to be a singer and dancer, and I was thrilled to bits. My first experience there, however, came as quite a shock.

Television House was a lovely old white-stone building in Richmond, an inner-city suburb of Melbourne, and that was where the classes took place. It was also where the production offices for the TV show were and where the rehearsals for the show were held, so everything was under one roof. At the back of the building there were two very large rooms: one for singing, and the other, which had a ballet barre and mirrors all along one wall, for dancing. The kids would go from one room to the other for their various lessons. All the action happened within these two rooms. Students would be dancing around, practising their demi-pliés or their tap steps, while their over-enthusiastic mothers sat at the tables, furiously sewing sequins onto elaborate stage outfits or fussing with ridiculous hairdos – it was quite an eye-opener.

Being new, I obviously wasn't expecting to be the best dancer or singer, but the first class I attended was full of kids my own age, about seven or eight, who already had what I thought was a wealth of experience. Some of them had old-fashioned stage mothers who really pushed them, painting make-up on them and constantly yelling at them to smile; then there were others who had already taken part in competitive shows and performed professionally and knew exactly what it meant to be a professional performer. I didn't know a thing! Still, I threw myself into it as best I knew how. After only a few weeks of classes, I was invited, along with my parents, to go and meet the famous Mr Johnny Young himself. We were asked if I'd like to appear on the show as one of the 'Tiny Tots'.

The Tiny Tots were a group of younger kids who featured principally as extras in big Christmas scenes, circus and fairground scenes, street scenes or whenever they needed to pad out the cast a bit. Apparently, my singing teacher at the school, Liana Scali, had singled me out to Johnny and the producers as someone to keep an eye on, but at seven I was much too young to be one of the full-time team members. Putting me in the Tiny Tots would give them a chance to find out how I came across on camera, how I coped in the studio and whether or not I had that special something they were always on the lookout for. Of course, at the time, I didn't know any of this – I was just excited to be going on the show, and maybe a little bit surprised. I knew I wasn't the best singer or the best dancer in my class by a long shot, but, as I found out later, being the prettiest or the most accomplished wasn't what *Young Talent Time* was about. Johnny wanted to find young performers with a certain kind of charisma who really connected with the show's wide-ranging television audience: kids who had qualities that other kids would love, and whom the mums and dads and grandmas would love too. Mum says she was always surprised they'd picked me as she didn't think I could sing.

'I guess you must have had something, though,' she muses now. 'The X factor, I suppose.'

Cheers, Mum!

*

Once I'd joined the Tiny Tots, there was absolutely no stopping me, and when Mum's sister mentioned that she knew of a female casting agent who was looking for kids to appear in various television shows, I begged Mum to take me along to meet her. Mum said, 'No!' She was dead against me going for auditions and castings when I was so young, and didn't want her children going into the entertainment business at all if she could possibly help it. Eventually, though, I wore her down with sweetness and good behaviour, and she agreed to take me to meet the casting agent on the condition that Brendan and Kylie came along to meet her too, just to make it fair.

It was an exciting day out for us kids. While we were at the offices, we answered questions, listed hobbies and had Polaroids taken while Mum filled out forms, and that was about all there was to it. I don't think Mum thought anything would come of it, to be honest. Then, Kylie got picked for the part of a little Dutch girl in *The Sullivans*, which was a popular period drama of the time. Soon after that, I was cast too, with a featured role in a show called *Skyways*, which was a Channel 7 soap opera set in an airport. I played a little girl who was smuggling her pet mouse aboard a plane to London, and I loved it. Then, like Kylie, I also got a small part in *The Sullivans*, which was exciting as it was such a big show back then. Kylie and I were both extremely happy that we'd been to see the casting agent that day. Mum still wasn't convinced, however.

On my eighth birthday, 20 October 1979, I appeared on *Young Talent Time* as one of the three contestants in the talent-quest section of the show. I sang 'On The Good Ship Lollipop' in a rather fetching sailor hat and nautical top that Nain had lovingly made for me, with my long brown hair tied in bunches. One of the judges, Evie Hayes, a respected grande dame of the theatre, proclaimed to the audience, 'Danielle is a darling little girl, who, with proper coaching and tuition, could have a very fine future.'

Well, I smiled vacantly and looked as cute as I possibly could, but I didn't really understand what she was saying, and I didn't win. Still, having experienced a brief moment under the glare of the studio spotlight, I now had the bug to perform and a determination that surprised everyone, including Mum and Dad. I wasn't thinking about being super-famous or being the all-out star of the show, I just wanted to be the absolute best that I could possibly be beneath those glorious lights. And yes, maybe I'd have to work harder than some of the other kids with their fancy costumes and their pushy stage-mums, but I'd get there in the end.

Back at the Minogue family home in Camberwell, things were as loud and hectic as they'd ever been. As we were growing up, Kylie, Brendan and I were all developing our own individual styles and tastes. Though we were never bad kids, I'm sure Mum and Dad must have had their hands full, given some of our antics. Brendan was into his rock music, and his room was a no-go area for us girls – a real boy's room, with posters of cars and his favourite band, KISS, all over the wall. He was still a daredevil too: now re-christened by Dad 'the Evel Knievel of Camberwell', a whole catalogue of bone fractures, bruises and other minor injuries befell my brother during our time at St John's Avenue. He'd gone over the handlebars of his bike more than once, and when he broke his arm in two different places, poor squeamish Mum almost fainted at the doctor's surgery and had to be helped onto the examination bed instead of her injured son. Then, one afternoon, Brendan came into the house screaming at the top of his lungs after crashing through a plate glass window while playing next door: he had glass embedded in his eyeballs! How Mum coped with all the constant blood and guts I'll never know. I'm not sure how I'll manage with one single drop of blood on my kid.

Kylie gave Mum the odd bit of trouble, too, as she blossomed into a teenager. One night, when Mum and Dad believed us all to be tucked up in bed, Kylie was, in fact, all done up in her spray-on skinny jeans and bright blue eyeliner, clambering out of the front window en route to the Golden Bowl for a secret liaison with her boyfriend. The Golden Bowl was a ten-pin bowling alley around the corner from us, and it was the cool place for teenagers to meet their friends, play pinball and smoke or 'pash', and do all those things young teenagers like to do but aren't supposed to. Now, this was a frightful dilemma for me, because I'd witnessed Kylie disappearing out of the window, and for that reason I knew I'd have to face the wrath of either Kylie or my mother. If I didn't spill my guts to Mum about her renegade eldest daughter, then I'd be in deep trouble once it came out that I'd known. However, if I did blab, I'd have to face an angry big sister and be labelled a tattle-tale. In the end, though, I was so terrified that something might happen to my big sister out on her own at night that I confessed to Mum what I knew and, of course, she was furious. It makes me laugh now when Mum tells the story of how she dashed straight over to the Golden Bowl and appeared at the top of the stairs, looming over poor Kylie like a big ogre and yelling, 'What the hell do you think you're doing? Get home this minute! OUT!'

A few days later while she was driving around the neighbourhood, Mum says she caught Kylie and her girlfriend Georgie wandering the local streets during school hours.

'We're on our way to the library!' Kylie had offered, meekly.

Mum was having none of it, though, and swung open the car door angrily.

'Get in the car right now, the pair of you! And Georgie, I'm ringing your mother!'

To this day, poor Kylie swears that she and Georgie were on their way to the library.

I, meanwhile, was getting a bit too old to be my brother's stunt double, but was still too young to be thinking about boys, so I concentrated on my singing and dancing, and gaining as much experience as I could from the talent school. I'd really enjoyed doing the little bit of acting that I'd done, but I was absolutely mad about music. I wasn't keen, though, on all the rock music that was blaring out of Brendan's room back then. By the time I was ten, I had my own favourite bands: I adored Culture Club and Wham!.

Every week, I would record all the songs that I loved from the chart countdown on my cassette recorder, obsessively making sure that I hit the pause button whenever the annoying ads came on; then I'd go back in my room, and play the recorded songs over and over again until I'd learned every single lyric and knew them all sideways and backwards. Every spare moment I had, in fact, was spent listening to pop music, practising my singing and dancing, or dressing up and performing for everyone in the lounge at our house in St John's Avenue.

Finally, all my hard work paid off, and in June 1982, on *Young Talent Time*'s special eleventh-birthday edition, I became a full-time team member, performing my first song, 'Who Wants To Be A Millionaire?'. Johnny Young, surrounded by the rest of the team, and as suave as ever in a tuxedo jacket and dickie bow, delivered a rousing build-up as he introduced a tiny, ten-year-old Danielle Minogue, dressed in a sweet blue-and-white frock. I sang the song alongside fellow newbie team member Mark McCormack. Now I really *was* on my way, regularly singing and dancing in the homes of millions of TV viewers . . . just like Olivia!

Chapter 4

Goodnight, Australia!

Being a regular team member on *Young Talent Time* was heaps of fun and a dream come true, but it was also incredibly hard work. It demanded a lot of commitment not just from me, but also from my whole family. Rehearsals for the show would be after school most days, and could finish any time from six in the evening until as late as ten at night. In those days, I didn't have my own driver ferrying me backwards and forwards to rehearsals; Mum or Dad had to take me there from school and then come and collect me again.

This often meant that family life at home could get a bit topsy-turvy, with dinner being delayed or poor Brendan and Kylie missing out on someone to help with their homework. For me, it meant hours and hours of extra work. All the kids on the show, like me, went to regular schools – there was no special tuition – so all week we had to find enough spare time to get all our homework assignments done, while attending every single rehearsal and learning all the songs and dance numbers for the live TV show on Saturday night.

It makes me smile now when I think about all the regulations there are for kids under seventeen working on TV shows like *The X Factor* and *Australia's Got Talent*. These days, there are quite rightly very strict rules about how many hours young people are allowed to work outside school, and if they *are* out of school for any amount of time, there are tutors and chaperones galore on hand to make sure they get their studying done. We had none of that back then; we finished at whatever hour we finished, and that was that.

The schedule went something like this: Monday, after school, we recorded all the vocals for the show. On Tuesday, again after school, I would squeeze in an extra singing lesson off my own back (I was well aware that I needed that little bit of extra tuition). Wednesday night we might have off, if there wasn't a photo shoot or something extra to do, and that's when I'd cram in most of my homework. Then on Thursday and Friday we'd dash straight from school to dance rehearsals at Television House. On Saturday – show day – we'd have twelve to thirteen hours of camera rehearsals for the actual show, which went live to air on a Saturday night.

The live show was, of course, the best part of the week and always a big thrill. At the top of the show, the entire team would come out to perform the big opening number, and I loved to hear the cheers and applause from the studio audience. Then, throughout the show, we'd all have our different solo spots or maybe a duet or two, and then we'd have the talent-quest section of the programme with Judges Ronnie Burns and Honor Walters. This was always fun, and saw kids with stars in their eyes from all over the country competing to be the best singer that week, with the added allure of a possible slot on a future show.

At the end of *Young Talent Time* each and every week, Johnny Young would come on and sing the Beatles' classic, 'All My Loving', in a lullaby style. All of us kids on the team would line up and sing along with him, swaying from side to side, while the studio audience swayed from side to side, and all the kids at home watching on television swayed from side to side. Then, as each team member in turn was captured on camera in a big, cheery close-up, Johnny Young would say with a smile, 'Goodnight, Katie . . . Goodnight, Vince . . . Goodnight, Karen . . . Goodnight, Danny . . .' and so on. (I was now known as Danny, with a 'y'.) At the close of every show, while the kids on the team grinned and waved to the viewers at home, Johnny would say, 'Goodnight, Australia!'

It sounds so cheesy now, but at the time the kids at home lapped it up. Hard work though it was, we knew how lucky we were. We somehow managed to get through each week, having a brilliant time along the way.

Working most days on a TV show like *Young Talent Time* was a bit like having another, rather extended family, and because I was at work so much, I probably saw them more than I did my real family. Johnny Young was very much the head of the clan. He was round faced and dark haired, and generally warm and smiley; his bright jackets and huge, wing-collared shirts from those days are legendary. We'd usually see Johnny only on Saturday afternoons, a few hours before the show went live, when he would breeze in and cast an eye over everything to ensure he was satisfied and make changes where he felt they were needed – very much like Simon Cowell might do on one of his shows now.

Being a staunch supporter of Essendon – an Aussie-rules football team nicknamed 'The Bombers' – Johnny would often be at one of their games before the Saturday show, sometimes taking a helicopter back from wherever they were playing to make it back in time. On those days, everybody in the studio, cast and crew alike, would be keeping a keen eye on the scores of the game, knowing full well that if his team lost, Johnny's usual bright mood would sour and it would be best to keep out of his way. Elements of the show that might not have bothered him at all on another day would suddenly become a huge problem on a day that 'The Bombers' had failed to make the grade – this musical number would be all wrong, or that scenery wouldn't be right. Of course, if they won, Johnny would be all sweetness and light and buzzing like mad when he walked into the studio ready for the evening's live broadcast.

I always found him very approachable. Being a reasonably confident girl, I was never put off by the fact that he was my boss and I was just a kid; I'd go straight to him with my own ideas for my numbers or outfits for the show. Of course, with my fervent eye for fashion I was quite vocal about what sort of styles I liked and, indeed, what songs I wanted to perform.

I knew exactly how I wanted to present myself as I entered my teenage years. This is the time when children really start to get a sense of who they are, and I was doing it in front of a million people every week. It had to be just right! Whereas some of the kids would rock up and put on the costumes they were given and do everything they were told, I remember having my 'producer's cap' on from a very young age, and would always be fussing around in the wardrobe room or stalking the studio floor, making all kinds of suggestions and probably getting on everybody's nerves.

'Why can't I wear something like this?' I'd say, holding a picture of Boy George or a young Madonna aloft. 'And I've seen this really cool camera angle in a pop video. Do you think we can copy it?'

Johnny Young reminds me now that I was always very determined and strong-minded, but I never thought about it back then. As far as I was concerned, I was a young girl with lots of wonderful ideas, and I wanted to get them out to whomever would listen.

Some of the ideas and 'looks' during my time on the show, however, are now grisly testament for all to behold: a canary-yellow-and-lime all-in-one bathing suit to perform the ELO song 'I'm Alive', with the *Young Talent Time* team and entire studio audience doing an aerobics routine all around me; a cerise pencil skirt and matching bat-winged top with white stilettos, topped with a fright-wig of frizzy, crimped hair to perform Diana Ross's 'Chain Reaction'; and a dress that made me look a bit like a Catholic monk in heels, which I tore off halfway through the second chorus of Madonna's 'Open Your Heart' to reveal a rather fetching tangerine mini-dress underneath. Adding insult to injury, this particular fabulous ensemble was complemented by a heavily lacquered quiff which probably helped start the hole in the O zone layer. Gorgeous!

At the time, I loved the dressing-up aspect of the show, and would always strive to avoid the customary sparkly camp clothes and go for the coolest or most way-out image I could concoct. Wild hairdos, bubble skirts and seasonal scenes painted on long fingernails at Christmas were the norm for me, and I'd proudly catwalk model each new get-up for my good friend Barbara, who ran the *Young Talent Time* wardrobe. She always encouraged me to be bold with my clothes, and couldn't wait to see what I'd come up with next.

We filmed most of the *Young Talent Time* programmes at the studios of ATV-10 in Nunawading, Melbourne. We were in studio A but, of course, there were other studios within the complex, and one of them, right down the corridor, was the home of the hit TV show *Prisoner*, known in the UK and America as *Prisoner Cell Block H*. Back then, *Prisoner* was a gritty drama series set in a tough women's prison; it has since become a campy, cult hit that spawned a stage musical. At one stage, our cast was sharing a green room with the ladies from *Prisoner* and we would all, at some point, pass through or hang out there while we were en route to the studio floor. There wasn't much in the green room, just a couple of couches down either side, but we'd often end up in there together: the ladies from the fictitious Wentworth Detention Centre in their austere blue prison attire and the kids from *Young Talent Time* in their sparkly, sequinned gowns and ridiculous costumes. One of the actresses from *Prisoner* would be sitting, studiously learning her lines, while next to her there was a giant lobster on one side and on the other a kid dressed up as a pineapple. The ladies were very courteous in front of us and there wasn't as much colourful language from them as there was from us kids. They did seem to like the booze and fags, though, and a few of the ladies kept bottles of gin stashed in their lockers in case of emergency.

One of the actresses was named Sheila Florence and she played a good-natured old jailbird called Lizzie in the series. Sheila was a lovely, gentle lady in her seventies who always sat in the same spot in the green room, and it seemed to me that she was the real matriarch of the cast. I never once saw Sheila without a lit cigarette. Quite a lot of the *Prisoner* women smoked but she really went for it, lighting one ciggie off the other; consequently, she had one of the most gravelly voices you're ever likely to hear. These days you can't smoke in any public buildings, yet there she was then puffing away like mad around a gaggle of young kids in highly flammable outfits. It's odd to think of it now.

As well as Barbara in wardrobe, who is still a close family friend today, there were plenty of other adults from the team whom I became close to back then: Maggie, the choreographer, and her husband, Ronnie, who was one of the judges; Greg, who became the show's musical director; and Bill, who did the make-up. Bill was wonderfully flamboyant, and he was great with all the kids. Although he let us muck around a bit, he didn't take any backchat, and he was always there when someone needed a shoulder to cry on or to pour out their heart. Let's face it, with a crowd of hormonal teenagers working the long hours we did, there was bound to be, and often were, a few tantrums and tears, and Bill would always be the best person to unburden yourself to. Although I'd heard people talking about the fact that Bill was gay, I didn't know what that meant when I was seven. All I knew was that Bill was funny and kind and that was enough for me. We spent hours cooped up in the make-up room with him over the years, and he always made it a fun place to be, coming up with the most ingenious ways of keeping everyone in line and all egos in check.

As well as a heart of gold, Bill had a whiplash tongue, and he had crafted a way to mince across a room like I've never seen since. He also, while entertaining everyone with his latest outlandish stories, managed to gesticulate while cocking an eyebrow and peering at you over the top of his glasses all at the same time – I thought this was utterly fabulous.

As time went on, I began taking an interest in something other than singing, dancing and fashion – boys! True, some of those who worked on the show could be quite annoying, especially when clambering out of their dressing room through the roof to catch a peek at us girls in our undies through a gap in the ceiling, but I started to pay a bit more attention to the opposite sex when I was about twelve or thirteen.

My first, and very innocent, crush was a boy called Vince Del Tito, who was a handsome, dark-haired boy almost exactly one year older than me. Like me, Vince had attended the Johnny Young Talent School and then graduated to the TV show, so we were already friends. During the run of one series, however, this friendship graduated to hand-holding in the studio, and on the tour bus whenever we performed around the country, and then to a kiss on the lips – my very first!

I didn't fare quite so well with some of the other boys. There was one called Bevan Addinsall who was utterly out of control and hyperactive; certain things he ate and drank sent him completely over the edge. Bevan was a good-looking boy with a fantastic voice. He got his spot on the *Young Talent Time* team after seeing an ad in the newspaper and auditioning against 5,000 other applicants, so was clearly very talented. If he managed to get his hands on any of the sugary goodies that triggered his over-energetic madness, however, there would be absolutely no calming him down.

He lived fairly close to me, so my parents and his would take it in turns to drive us both to and from the studios or rehearsals. That was anything up to six nights a week, so Bevan and I spent a lot of time together – perhaps a little too much. Being an only child, and having just moved to Melbourne from out in the sticks, the excitement of being around loads of other kids and a TV studio was often too much for Bevan. He could never concentrate for more than about five min-utes. He would tear around everywhere, disappearing and running amok unless his feet were virtually nailed to the floor. This used to drive everyone up the wall, of course, especially me, as I prided myself on being very focused and always strove to concentrate on the job at hand. Whenever the rest of us were trying to get on with something impor-tant, at some point there would invariably be the cry of 'Where's Bevan?' and we'd have to wait until he'd been duly located and dragged back to wherever he was supposed to be.

One afternoon during dance rehearsals at Television House, Bevan finally crossed the line with me. He'd been taunting and annoying me all day while I was trying to practise a routine, forcing me to issue him with a stern threat.

'Bevan, I've had enough. If you don't go away and leave me alone, you're gonna get it!'

To be honest, I had absolutely no idea what I was going to do if he ignored me and carried on – I guess I thought the threat would be enough. But, of course, it wasn't enough, and back he came to taunt me again and again while I was trying to concentrate. I don't really know what happened next. Somewhere from within my little frame, this ball of energy and fury fused together and my arm left the side of my body, fist tightly clenched, and connected with Bevan's face – hard. I'd never thrown a punch before, and didn't think I even knew how, but poor Bevan fell like a tree in front of all the other astonished kids, who looked on, completely agog. I was in shock too, but knew that somehow I'd have to follow through with my bolt-from-the-blue tough-guy act, so I puffed my chest out, dusted my hands together and said, with as much bravado as I could muster, 'Right, that'll be the last time you do that, then, Bevan!' and walked off.

This event transformed my previously rocky relationship with Bevan. Eventually, believe it or not, he became like another brother to me. We've stayed friends to this day, and I occasionally visit him and his wife and two children in Queensland. He's still a singer and performer too, and by family request sang at my grandmother's ninetieth birthday in 2009.

When I was about fifteen and becoming a young woman, one of my other male friends from the show, Joey Perrone, brought his pal from Sydney along to the studio. The friend's name was Gary. He was a striking blond Italian boy with full lips and a strong Roman nose, and I was quite taken with him . . . OK, he was hot! Some of us from the team would socialise outside work, and one sunny afternoon, a whole gang of us, including Joey and his gorgeous friend Gary, went horse riding in the country. As usual, we all had a great time together, and as the day wore on it became more and more obvious that Gary was just as smitten with me as I was with him. We laughed and talked as we drifted leisurely through the beautiful open countryside on our horses, both realising that this was most definitely the start of something.

The only problem was geography. Once we were going steady, Gary would drive all the way down to Melbourne from Sydney to spend time with me whenever he could, and I'd visit him and his wonderful

Italian family in his home town, where he'd take me waterskiing and on romantic dates by the sea. We both had our own lives and work to get on with in different cities, and it was hard being apart for as much time as we were. This wasn't the innocent, holding-hands type of romance I'd had with Vince – Gary was my first real boyfriend. I'd fallen in love for the first time, which can be pretty intense when you're fifteen, and talking on the phone just wasn't the same. I missed him terribly when he wasn't around.

The long-distance relationship has been a recurring theme in my love life. There was Julian in New York, Steve in LA and Kris in Manchester, and me in a different city – or country. I'll save all that for later, but suffice it to say that in those circumstances both parties have to be really strong if they want to keep the flame alight. Sadly, as in the case of gorgeous Gary and me, it often just flickers out.

Sometimes, the team members' families would feature in skits or 'up close and personal' sections of the show. I once had the whole camera crew round at our place in St John's Avenue, giving the TV audience a guided tour of the Minogue household and everyone who lived there – even our dog, Gabby, appeared on *Young Talent Time*.

It suddenly dawned on me that I was now quite famous. At my school, Camberwell High, I would notice some of the other kids whispering or making the odd remark about me as they passed me in the corridor. I'd ignore them most of the time and hang out with my best friend, Alethia. Of course, having big brother Brendan and his mates at the same school and looking out for me was always a great deterrent for any potential tormentor.

When *Young Talent Time* toured the country, playing shopping malls and arenas across Australia, it really hit home how famous we were. Thousands of kids from every area would turn up to see the live shows and they'd go nuts. There was one horrible incident in a Sydney shopping centre, which turned into a virtual riot, with something like 17,000 fans all surging forward to get a bit closer to their favourite team member. It was terrifying for us, and a few of the audience there that day were injured.

In 1985, Johnny Young introduced my sister, Kylie, on the live show. She was starring in a brand-new Aussie show called *The Henderson Kids* and becoming quite the actress – I was very proud. A year later, she was back on the show performing a duet with me, which was amazing for us after all those years of performing together for Mum and Dad in the lounge at home. It was a big moment in *Young Talent Time* history too. Kylie had just landed the television role that would change her life: playing the part of feisty car mechanic Charlene Robinson in *Neighbours*. We strutted out on stage in matching silver dresses with tons of eighties poodle hair and performed a cover of the song 'Sisters Are Doing It For Themselves'. There was no doubt about it – we absolutely were!

In April 1998, when I finally bowed out of *Young Talent Time* at the age of sixteen, there were lots of tears. Vince Del Tito helped me choose my final song, which was 'How Do You Keep The Music Playing?' by the composer Michel Legrand. My mum and Kylie were in the studio audience, along with hundreds of tearful fans holding up posters of me. In fact, by the time I'd got halfway through the song, all the team, girls and boys, were in absolute floods and I could barely make it to the end. I was wearing a bottle-green silk, strapless gown and my hair was swept up in a demure, Audrey Hepburn-style beehive. As I sang, a waterfall of silver confetti fell around me – very dramatic stuff! When I finished the song, I broke down completely, with Johnny and all the team lovingly surrounding me. In the dying seconds of my final *Young Talent Time*, I got to say the famous closing line of the show: 'Goodnight, Australia!'

It was then that a message flashed across the screens of TV sets all over the country. It said: 'Goodbye and good luck . . . DANNII.'

Chapter 5

A Knack for Negotiating

I am absolutely shocking at ball sports and always have been. I cannot throw or catch a ball. In fact, if any terrifying, fast-moving spherical object comes my way even now, I'll wave my hands in the air and scream like a banshee rather than attempt to catch it. This had ruled out most of the PE curriculum at Camberwell High apart from swimming, which is the one sport I loved, especially as it gave me the opportunity for a bit of sun-baking around the wonderful outdoor Olympic-sized pool adjacent to the school. Anyway, with all the work I had on with the TV show, plus all the homework being piled on us by the teachers every week, something had to give – and I had a plan.

Mr Anderson was the games teacher, and he was a good guy with a great sense of humour. The kids liked him because he didn't talk down to them, and they respected him because he was firm but fair. One morning, when I was about fourteen years old, I strode up to Mr Anderson in my little green-and-white-checked school uniform and announced: 'Sir, I'd really like to discuss something with you if that's OK. Can we set up a meeting?'

I can see myself standing there in the school corridor, shoulder-length brown hair with blonde highlights and a spiky fringe, with sparkly blue eyes – by this time I'd even grown into my teeth. Mr Anderson nodded, slightly bewildered, and when we finally sat down, I put my case forward.

'You and I both know that I can't do ball sports,' I said. 'It's not me, Mr Anderson. It is never gonna happen. You also know that I have a full-time job after school, which is five or six days a week, so it's very difficult to find the time to do homework.'

Mr Anderson nodded again, still bemused. I went on.

'You've seen my report card, and how studious I am: all of my other subjects are either 'A' or 'A-plus', but I'll be lucky if I get a 'D' in PE the way I'm going this year, right?'

More nodding.

'So here's the deal I'm proposing: I get lots of exercise with all the dancing I do, and I'm happy to stick with the swimming, but other than that, if your lessons are going to involve me running in the opposite direction whenever a scary ball comes at me, then I'd be better off in the library working hard on all my other subjects to keep those grades as good as they are now, don't you think? Fail me now at PE, and let's just call it a day. I'll have more time to get all my other homework done, and you won't have to hear me screaming every time there's a netball game on – everybody wins!'

Well, as I said, Mr Anderson was firm but always very fair, and I never played another ball game at school. Job done!

Towards the end of my run on *Young Talent Time*, I'd had a lot of fan mail about the wild and wonderful stage clothes and costumes I'd worn on the show, and Kmart, the department-store chain, approached me about the idea of coming up with my own fashion range for young people. I was over the moon, as fashion design was something I was really keen to try. I knew I'd have a real blast working with professional designers to come up with some fresh, new ideas for kids' clothes.

By this time in Australia I was well known as 'Dannii'– finally having settled on the double 'N' and double 'I' simply because nobody else spelled it that way, and I decided that was what I wanted to call my clothing range too. I was very eager to get started with the designs. I knew the clothes had to be practical, not too elaborate and, of course, nothing like some of the stagy get-ups I'd worn on *Young Talent Time*. I felt I had an instinct about what kids my age would or wouldn't like, so I kept that in mind all the time I was working with the designers. Luckily, my instincts were right: when the first Dannii fashion range sold out in a record ten days in the spring of 1988, I was ecstatic.

While all this was going on, Dad suggested I might need a manager to look after me. Kylie had taken on a manager from Melbourne called Terry Blamey, and her career was exploding. She'd been a big hit in *Neighbours*, and her pop career was taking off too. She'd signed a deal with Mushroom Records in Australia and had a huge hit with a cover of 'The Loco-Motion'. Her next single was 'I Should Be So Lucky' which was, of course, absolutely massive all over Europe. The rest is pop history!

Dad thought it would be a good idea if I met with Terry, with a view to him managing my career, even though I wasn't sure exactly what that was going to be. Yes, I was still passionate about music, but I wanted to finish my studies and then perhaps go to a technical college or film school so I could learn how to be a director. I'd spent so much of my youth in television studios and was fascinated by what went on behind the scenes, it seemed a sensible progression to me. Few *Young Talent Time* team members had gone on to have professional singing careers after they'd left the show – why should I be the exception?

Over the years, people have always said to me things like: 'Dannii, you must have been so ambitious as a child,' or 'I guess you were driven to be successful because your sister was.' The idea that I'm very competitive and ambitious is one of the biggest misconceptions about me and it makes me smile when I think of it now. The truth of the matter was I had no vision, no target and absolutely no game plan. Ever since I was little I'd loved performing and I'd been lucky to grow up doing just that on TV.

After a couple of meetings with Terry Blamey, both Dad and I decided that he was the right man for the job. He was taking Kylie's career from strength to strength and was obviously well connected in the entertainment industry. He played a big part in setting up the Dannii clothing range deal with Kmart, and suggested that he had big musical plans for me too. I had no idea what other sorts of opportunities were going to arise and, to tell you the truth, I was just going with the flow.

Terry was a smart cookie, though, and had the idea of taking me to meet Michael Gudinski, who ran Mushroom Records and had originally signed Kylie after hearing her sing at a benefit concert with some of the other *Neighbours* cast members a couple of years earlier. Terry's thinking was that I was already famous and popular all over Australia as a singer on TV, so why not make a pop record? If people were snatching the Dannii clothing range off the shelves as fast as they were, why wouldn't they do the same with a Dannii album? Gudinski wasn't really a 'pop' man back then, and definitely favoured rock music, but he and his right-hand man, Gary Ashley, agreed with Terry. In January 1989, I was offered, against all my expectations, my very first recording contract. Everyone around me was very excited, but no one was more surprised than I was.

Whenever Kylie was home, it was thrilling to hear about all the exotic places she'd been. Dad had taken us all on a wonderful trip to Europe, Canada and California a few years earlier, but Kylie had been to Tokyo and New York, and places that I dreamed of going one day. Every time she unpacked her suitcases, I'd peer over the edge, wide-eyed at some of the weird and fabulous gadgets and trinkets she'd brought from places like Japan, never really believing that I'd eventually go there too.

Mum and Dad were always so happy when she was home too. Being the parents they are, and the family we are, nothing important ever changed. Although they now had a world-famous daughter, they took it in their stride and tried to keep our family life as happy and as natural as it had always been. They'd been exactly the same when I was on *Young Talent Time*: yes, I was dressed up in a posh frock, singing and dancing on TV sets all over the country every Saturday night, but once

I was back home, I was just Ron and Carol's little girl, Danielle. This, during some of the events that were to come in later years, is what kept us grounded.

Imagine Mum and Dad's surprise, though, a few months later when I told them that my A&R man at Mushroom Records had decided that my debut album would be recorded in . . . New York City!

When Gary Ashley met with Terry Blamey and me to discuss the album, he told us that if we were going to do this, it had to be right.

'Dannii needs her own sound,' he said. 'I've met these great pop writer-producers in New York who would be perfect. Dannii should go and record the record there.'

Mum, once again, was the voice of reason.

'But I thought you wanted to carry on with your studies,' she said as I sat down with her and Dad to discuss this awesome proposition.

'Well, why don't I give it a year?' I suggested. 'If it doesn't work out, then I'll go back to studying. I'm not expecting anything big to come of it anyway, but I'd be mad not to give it a go now it's been offered. Even if I do just one album, it'll be a great experience.'

Poor Mum – she hadn't wanted me or Kylie to go into the entertainment business when we were young, and now she had one daughter who'd spent the last six years on the country's top variety show, and another who was a famous pop star travelling all over the world and hardly ever home. My brother Brendan, at least, had decided on a career behind the camera, not in front of it, but even he ended up travelling around the world for months on end as an award-winning news cameraman for Channel 9 in Australia. Still, after much enthusiastic urging from me, both Mum and Dad finally agreed to it.

'Your grades at school were always good,' Mum said, 'so I guess I can't really argue with you trying this out for a year.'

My dazzling negotiating skills had been put to good use once more. I was off to the Big Apple, baby . . .

Chapter 6

Strewth! Where the Bloody Hell Are We?

When the yellow taxi turned the corner, the whole of Manhattan rose up before me under a bright blue sky. It was an incredible moment. New York City has been such an iconic setting for so many movies, TV shows and photographs, you almost feel like you know it before you get there. My eyes were everywhere as the cab snaked along the streets. As I was only seventeen, my A&R man, Gary Ashley, had come along on the trip to look after me and make sure the recording sessions went smoothly, and also to set me up in an apartment. My own apartment in Manhattan – woooooooooooow!

It was the summer of 1989, and Soul II Soul's 'Keep On Movin'' seemed to be pumping out of every car stereo. I was captivated by New York from the moment I arrived. There was an energy and buzz about the place that was completely contagious. The myriad different faces, the clothes, the noise and the smells – even the steam rising up out of the manhole covers and drains – were mesmerising to me. It was a whole world away from the calm quiet of the Melbourne suburbs I'd left behind. When we reached the huge building that housed my apartment in the heart of Midtown, I was again knocked for six. 'It's the Trump Tower!'

When I walked through the doors and clapped eyes on the ostentatious pink marble and gold and mirrored walls of the lobby, I could hardly believe my eyes. There was even a waterfall that cascaded down a wall of mosaic marble bricks into a pool below. What's more, I was escorted upstairs and shown into a massive, beautiful two-bedroom apartment. I couldn't get my head around the fact that for the next month or so I was going to be recording my own album with a New York production team and living in my very own apartment in the Trump Tower.

I got used to the city very quickly. People had said to me that you either love it or hate it when you first arrive – I was in love with it. I'd walk out of my apartment each bright morning and watch the horses and carriages ferrying tourists around Central Park, where people were doing all those very American things that I'd always imagined they would be: catching Frisbees, playing baseball and buying oversized pretzels and Dr Pepper from the carts of various vendors. I'd walk past the Plaza Hotel, which I'd seen in a ton of famous movies, and, of course, Tiffany's is right next door to the Trump Tower.

My producers were Alvin Moody and Vinnie Bell, who had worked with artists such as Whitney Houston and Neneh Cherry. Our first meeting with them was going to be at Alvin's studio in the Bronx. Gary and I got ourselves ready, then hailed a cab outside the building, but the driver who stopped wouldn't take us. We tried another cab with the same result, and then another. None of the yellow taxis would take us to our meeting in that part of the Bronx. That didn't sound so good to me.

'Ah! No, it's fine – perfectly safe!' Alvin assured the two of us anxious Aussies when we called him. So Gary and I took a private-hire car with a driver out to the Bronx, exchanging nervous glances as we went. Our driver explained that some of the taxi drivers were feeling a bit apprehensive about that area of the Bronx at the moment. Apparently, a couple of cab drivers had recently been shot and killed very near the address that we needed to get to; even if we'd found a taxi to take us there, we'd never have found one to bring us back. When we arrived at what we thought was our destination, Gary and I got out of the car. 'Strewth! Where the bloody hell are we?'

We weren't quite where we needed to be. The two of us fretfully headed up the few blocks towards Alvin's place, sticking out like a sore thumb in that neighbourhood. We were two fresh-off-the-boat Aussies with broad accents trying to navigate our way around the big bad Bronx. Now it seems hysterically funny, but at the time I was petrified.

Alvin and Vinnie were great, though, and I clicked with them right away. We'd already heard a demo song that they'd written before we left Australia: it was called 'Love And Kisses' and I thought it was perfect. They had some other songs that I was excited about, too, like 'Work' and 'Call To Your Heart' – great pop dance songs that I could see myself performing. I would get the chance to co-write some lyrics myself as the sessions progressed.

We were recording at the Greene Street Studio in the heart of SoHo in Manhattan. Once Gary had settled me in and gone back to Melbourne, I'd walk there alone from the apartment every day, which was quite a trot. I felt comfortable, almost at home, and even though I was still a wide-eyed Aussie girl in the fast-moving metropolis, it certainly wasn't the scary place that I thought it might be. I wanted to soak up the whole vibe of the city while I was there and take in as much as I could; plus, with all the amazing food I was enjoying, I needed the exercise!

One day while on a wander, I discovered the fabulous boutique owned by Patricia Field, who is now famous for her work as a costume designer on *Sex and the City* and *The Devil Wears Prada*, and I bought myself the coolest cropped black leather jacket with 'tattoo-painted' sleeves, and a gold crucifix necklace, both of which I ended up wearing in my very first video for the single 'Love And Kisses'.

Once at the studio, Alvin, Vinnie and I had many laughs: they were both hilariously funny guys and so enthusiastic. Sure, it was hard work, because we had to get as much done on the album as we could in only a few weeks, but they were both easy to work with, which was quite a relief as the studio sessions were often long ones. We'd end up having almost all our meals – lunch and dinner on most days – ordered in from the great array of diners and restaurants around SoHo. It suited me: at seventeen I was still four years below the legal drinking age in America, so I couldn't go out partying anyway. You couldn't get into most clubs and bars without ID, let alone drink. My tipples were Snapple iced tea, and cinnamon coffee from the coffee shop down the block – divine!

So Alvin, Vinnie and I were pretty much in a world of our own, jamming in the studio and making music. The best part of it was that they didn't know me from a bar of soap. I had none of the 'child star from *Young Talent Time*' baggage when I walked into their world every day; I was just a fresh new potential pop star straight out of the box. I felt completely free. The recording sessions went brilliantly, and it was decided at the end of the trip that I would come back again to record more, once Alvin and Vinnie had written the songs for me.

The following month back home in Melbourne felt desperately quiet by comparison. I missed the constant buzz of Manhattan terribly, but I knew that the work I'd done with the boys so far was great, and I couldn't wait to hear the finished mixes. They were going for a real American pop dance feel, which I was into at the time. I had the rest of the album and my first video to look forward to as well.

There was something more immediate on the horizon, however. Some time before the New York trip, I'd been asked to audition for a part in the Australian soap *Home and Away*. The show was becoming more and more popular, and, like *Neighbours*, was also doing well in the UK. At that point, I wasn't going to pass up any opportunity that came my way: the more auditions I did, the more experience I'd be gaining as an actress. When I read for the part of the character Marilyn, though, I remember thinking that the role wasn't right for me, and sure enough I didn't get it. After meeting me that day, however, the producers approached Terry Blamey with the idea of writing a part in the show especially for me.

What they came up with was a character called Emma Jackson, a rude, rebellious, troubled teen with an almost punk image – the absolute opposite of my quirky but wholesome *Young Talent Time* persona. Of course, I loved it right away. There were just a couple of problems to overcome: for one thing, I was still in the middle of record-ing an album and at some point would have to fly back to New York; and secondly – and this was the thing that scared me – it meant moving to Sydney, which was the setting and backdrop for the fictional town of Summer Bay, for a year.

No, I couldn't possibly do that. I'd committed to recording my album and I was going to see it through. Terry came up with the idea that I should do a short run on the show to see how it went – thirteen weeks to be exact – with an option to extend if all went well. That way I could go back and get the album done when I'd finished filming, and not miss out on what could be a great opportunity as an actress.

Leaving my family and moving all the way to Sydney to work on a soap opera and then flying back and forth to America to finish my album – could I possibly do it all? It seemed completely inconceivable. For a start, I'd have to get my driver's licence – *Home and Away* was shot in two completely separate locations that were quite far apart. I'd also have to find somewhere to live, as I certainly didn't want to be stuck in a hotel for all that time. My life would be turned upside down. Since leaving *Young Talent Time* and not having a clue what I was going to do next, suddenly – and this has been a recurring theme in my profes-sional life – there was a lot going on.

Chapter 7

It's Always Summer in Summer Bay

Everything seemed to be one big crazy rush once I'd agreed to take the part of Emma Jackson in *Home and Away*, as filming was starting in a matter of weeks. Mum and Dad seemed happy enough about me dashing off to Sydney – after all, it was just for thirteen weeks, right? Wrong. When my character, Emma, proved a big hit with audiences across Australia, I ended up staying for the full year that the producers had originally offered.

Terry Blamey's brother, Ted, solved the problem of where I was going to live. He had a friend called Marissa who rented a house in Neutral Bay, which is over the Sydney Bridge on the North Shore. Palm Beach, where the location shots for the programme were filmed, was up the coast further north, and Epping, where the studio shoots were done, was inland, so there was a fair distance between them. Neutral Bay seemed a good spot for me, and I certainly didn't feel ready to live on my own in a strange city.

Mum and Dad, too, were anxious about my living arrangements. 'We'd like to meet Marissa before you move in with her, of course,' Dad told me.

I think it was to make sure she wasn't a wild party girl, to be honest, but Marissa was a mature young woman in her mid-twenties who took the ferry across the harbour every day to a respectable banking job in the city, and was a terrific girl. She wore smart suits, stockings and pearls to work, and she was very responsible, so when Mum and Dad went up to visit her, they came away happy.

It was fortunate for me, too, that I didn't end up rooming with another seventeen-year-old like me. Never having had to look after myself, I had absolutely no idea what to do when all these cryptic letters addressed to me started to arrive through the post.

'Marissa, what on earth is this?' I remember saying to her, waving the bizarre document under her nose.

'It's a telephone bill, Dannii!' she'd explain.

Having already been married and divorced, Marissa was worldly like that.

When I got to the Channel 7 studios to prepare for the part of Emma, I was happy to discover that the producers wanted me to go for it. The interesting thing about having Dannii Minogue on the show, as far as they were concerned, was to take the character as far away as possible from the all-singing, all-dancing, sweet, smiling girl that people knew from *Young Talent Time*. And that's what made it interesting and worthwhile for me: I was thrilled with the leather jacket and the full-on make-up because it was so different to anything I'd done before.

The surly, dark, punk Emma Jackson was the first impression that the British public had of me: I was known as a tough, cool, rebellious teen, full of angst. In Australia, they could still remember me dressed as a pineapple. The role was also a complete contrast to Kylie's portrayal of bubbly Charlene in *Neighbours*, and that's what Channel 7 also wanted – an explosive character that *Home and Away* hadn't seen before.

For the first couple of weeks working on set, I have to admit I felt very homesick, and I missed my family and friends terribly. Sydney is a great city but it has a very different vibe to Melbourne. At first, I found it hard going, despite the fact that I'd felt at home on the other side of the world in New York. There were a lot of other *Home and Away* cast members around the same age as me. When I first got there, they knew exactly who I was but I didn't know any of them, so I didn't feel part of the gang. I felt they saw me as the girl from *Young Talent Time* who'd had a role created especially for her and was sure to get special treatment. After all, I hadn't rocked up to a cattle-call audition and won the role; it had been handed to me on a plate.

This uneasiness was compounded by the fact that because I still couldn't drive when I first arrived, I had cars provided to shuttle me back and forth between locations and to and from home, while everyone else was expected to get around under their own steam. Even at weekends, when some of the other cast members would hang out together, I'd travel all the way back to Melbourne to be with my family because I was so homesick. To be honest, none of the other teenage cast members was ever mean to me, and things got better as time went on and I became more established, but I felt there were a few sideways glances and an air of 'who does she think *she* is' in the early days.

Two people I did click with right away, and consequently adored, were Judy Nunn and Ray Meagher, who played Ailsa and Alf Stewart. They were two of the older members of the cast and were just gorgeous to me on set during the first couple of weeks of filming when I was more than a little nervous. After all, this was the biggest acting job I'd had and I didn't want to disappoint. The filming of the scenes seemed to move very quickly, and everyone knew exactly what they were doing except me. It took me a while to get the hang of hitting marks on certain words to get the desired camera shot exactly right, with no shadow from the lights. Judy and Ray, though, were eager for me to feel comfortable and settled in those first weeks, so they would engage me in chitchat between takes to keep me relaxed. I expect they could see the fear in my eyes.

Ray is a sweet, gentle man who was loved by everyone working on the show. His character, Alf, would make me chuckle with lines such as 'Stone the crows' or 'Ya flaming Galah' (this is Aussie slang for idiot, and comes from the native Australian bird of the same name). Judy, meanwhile, is an accomplished author as well as an actress, and I remember her working on her books between takes. She kept all her notes and manuscripts stashed behind the bar at the Summer Bay diner.

Unlike the teenagers in the show, who were understandably excited about being newly famous and on the cover of this teen magazine or that, Ray and Judy were seasoned actors, and I suppose I related to them more because I'd already been through all the excitement of being on television every week. At the tender age of seventeen I was, absurdly, already an old hand, despite my initial jitters.

I also grew fond of little Katie Ritchie, who played Sally, and of Craig McLaughlin, who played the part of schoolteacher Grant 'Mitch' Mitchell. He had previously played Kylie's brother in *Neighbours*, and he had the most evil and contagious sense of humour on set, which often got me into trouble. If I was doing a close-up shot and Craig was off camera but in my sightline, he would pull a ridiculous face or do something infantile to get me to crack up laughing and ruin the shot. Of course, I would be the one in hot water with the director.

None of the crew wanted to have to shoot scenes over and over again. Still, Craig would get you every time, even if everyone was tired and wanted to go home. He did it all in such good spirits, simply wanting to keep people smiling, that even when everyone was pissed off, they'd still end up falling about laughing at his antics. He was absolutely brilliant to work with.

Work days were long and hard on *Home and Away*, and often utter madness. I'd find myself dashing from the location site to film one scene in a bikini, then back to the studio to film another scene in my school uniform. Palm Beach, where all the main location stuff was filmed, is a gorgeous beachside suburb about 40 kilometres north of Sydney. With its golden sands and beautiful azure water, it's always been a Mecca for surfers and sailors. It was a fabulous drive up the coast from where I lived in Neutral Bay. On days when I was filming there, I'd often arrive before sunrise, desperate to get to the catering van with all its steaming hot drinks and tasty breakfasts, especially in the winter months. Then I'd stand and watch the sun drift up over the wild surf, clutching a much needed cup of coffee and think: 'This is the best job in the world!'

This early-morning euphoria wore thin after eight hours of standing in the drizzling rain in a minuscule swimsuit and thongs (flip flops). The rain had to be really heavy for filming to be halted, and if you had to walk along the beach in a light downpour, so be it! One of the crew would hurtle alongside you with a screen to make sure your face didn't get too wet and show the rain on camera.

We'd all spot lines in the script, such as 'Let's go for a swim', which, in the winter months, filled us with utter dread. On one particularly arctic morning, I approached one of the producers with what I felt was a practical initiative, given the unmistakable drop in temperature.

'I know I'm supposed to be in a bikini today,' I said, breezily, 'and that's fine, but could I maybe pop a little shirt or a cardigan over the top of it?'

He looked at me as if I might have lost my mind.

'No, Dannii,' he said. 'It's always summer in Summer Bay.'

They knew their market well. *Home and Away* was now huge in the UK, and one of its major selling points was that it was chock-o-block with gorgeous, sun-kissed Aussie teenagers tearing around a beautiful beach in a state of semi-undress. I had no idea how popular the show had become in Britain. The public there were enjoying soaking up a bit of what us Aussies took for granted, and it was bringing in the big bucks.

Despite the show's popularity, Channel 7 seemed to be feeling the pinch of recession, and every week there seemed to be another few cutbacks made, and fewer crew members to say 'G'day' to. All the crew, in fact, were constantly making jokes about the very real possibility of getting fired from their jobs at the channel, as times were so tough. One such gag was cheekily circulated on *Home and Away*-headed notepaper, with the production-office details in the top right-hand corner. I discovered it stuck to the front of my script folder:

As you know, we had planned to have our previously cancelled

Xmas party under the Wisteria arbour in The Eastwood Hall. This was replaced by our subsequently cancelled Xmas party, which was to have taken place next to the ladies' dressing room – by the pile of empty 'spring water' bottles. However, due to a managerial oversight and a small financial glitch, all of the above are now replaced by a free pizza of your own choice (small) or two spring rolls per artist, available only from studio '0' on 31 December at 4a.m. . . . B.Y.O.

There was also a note stuck up on our green-room noticeboard. It was again written on Channel 7-headed paper, and had a gold dagger attached to it with a Channel 7 logo on it. The note read: '*Available now! The hand-finished Channel 7 dagger. To be worn between the shoulder blades (or bum cheeks.)*'

I guess the tight budget explained why the sets looked like cardboard when you got up close to them – they were all propped up with sandbags and stands at the back.

There was one person in the cast of *Home and Away* who would one day change my life but, of course, I couldn't have known it then. His name was Julian McMahon. Julian was the six-foot-two, brown-haired, blue-eyed son of the former Australian Prime Minister, William McMahon, but he'd also been a model in a Levi's jeans TV advertisement, which was much more of a big deal to me at the time. He was charismatic and funny and seemed to get on well with most of the other cast members and, I have to admit, I was somewhat bowled over when I met him.

Julian knew how to work a room: if he was around, you always knew it, and not in an annoying, showy way either. He was charming and witty, and loved nothing more than to entertain people and make them happy. As far as I was concerned, that was a nice sort of person to be around. Sometimes, Julian would be quite flirty with me but, to be perfectly honest, he flirted with absolutely everyone, so I didn't think it was any big deal and played along innocently, with nothing ever coming of it – at least not then anyway. I liked the fact that, much like Craig McLaughlin, he wanted to make people laugh, which, of course, meant he was usually the centre of attention – a typical Leo. Although we didn't have any storylines or scenes together on the show, Julian McMahon was definitely on my radar.

Thinking back on some of the storylines and scenes – especially the more meaty ones – I *did* have on *Home and Away*, though, makes me smile. My character, Emma Jackson, a wayward teen taken in by Ray and Judy's characters, Alf and Ailsa, could be a real tough bitch, and was great to play – she was always the bad girl. My arch-nemesis in the show was a character called Vicky Baxter, played by Nana Coburn. Vicky was also not a very nice young lady, and I had some great scenes with her, including the classic cat-fight at the bus stop after school, with tons of arm twisting and hair pulling; I even got to dump a milkshake over her head in the diner, though I can't for the life of me remember what flavour it was.

Emma ruined the Summer Bay beauty contest by parading up and down in vile clothes with hideous make-up. She had decided that beauty pageants were sexist and degrading to women, and said as much to the assembled crowd. The contest was won by the character Marilyn, who was the Summer Bay bimbo, and the part I'd originally read for but didn't get. I guess it was pretty obvious that I'd ended up with the right role for me: the feisty tomboy was always going to be so much more fun to play than the dizzy blonde!

Things started to go well for me once my character was established in *Home and Away*. In September 1989, the second Dannii clothing range sold out in record time again, and at the end of the year everyone at Channel 7 was over the moon when an Australian magazine called *TV Hits* voted me 'New Star of 1989'. I was an excited teenager! Then, early in 1990, things started to rev up even more. Mushroom Records decided to release my debut single in Australia before the album was finished. After all, I was appearing on television every night as a popular character in one of the country's hottest shows – I guess it would have been mad for them not to take advantage of that.

'Love And Kisses' was released in February, and climbed the charts to number four. I was overjoyed. My song was in the top five – it was almost too much to take in. Suddenly, I was flying all over the place to do radio and TV promotion for a hit single while still working on *Home and Away*. Though I loved every minute of it, it was exhausting; I wasn't getting nearly enough sleep.

I'd taken time off from the show to do a video clip for the song, and as usual wanted to be involved in absolutely every aspect of the process. I worked with the directors, Paul Goldman and Craig Griffin, on the storyboard, had a hand in auditioning the dancers and even chose my own clothes – including the fabulous leather jacket and gold cross I'd bought at Patricia Field in New York. It was the era of white faces and bright red lips, so I remember caking on the pale foundation to cover up my beautiful, bronze tan to get the desired look for the shoot.

The whole thing felt great – it felt like *me*! I was finally stepping into my own skin. The thrill of meeting so many new and talented people was electric. Whether they were producers, dancers, stylists or make-up people, I learned so much from them all and soaked up every new experience like a sponge. When I look back on that time now, I see one big explosion of fun, colour and vibrancy.

After the success of 'Love And Kisses', I had to take a short sabbatical from *Home and Away* to go back to New York and finish the album. It was wonderful to be back in my favourite city with Alvin and Vinnie, making music again. With the chart success of my single, I felt relaxed and confident that we'd laid the foundations of something great. While we were beavering away one day, I got a call from Australia: it was my A&R man, Gary Ashley.

'You've gone gold,' he said with excitement. '"Love And Kisses" has gone gold!'

My first single had sold over 35,000 copies in Australia and everyone at the studio was ecstatic. This fabulous news inspired Alvin and me to write the song 'Success', which eventually became my second single.

By then, I knew for sure that it was time for me to leave *Home and Away* and concentrate on the upcoming release of my album. True, I'd be leaving a stable job with good money, and I'd certainly miss some of the friends I'd made, but the days had started to feel so repetitive in comparison to all the different experiences I was having with music, and I hated being away from my friends and family in Melbourne. It seemed like there was nothing left for me to learn on the show, so I made a decision to say goodbye before I started hating it. I left Summer Bay how I'd like to remember it – always summer.

Chapter 8

Fish and Chips and Lori Lipkies

Lori Lipkies was about the most glamorous thing I'd ever seen: tall, with long, wild curly hair and always, *always*, fire-engine red lipstick, coupled with long, perfectly manicured matching red nails. She would wear the finest clothes from Europe, and she seemed to have a glamorous lifestyle like nobody else I knew – with gorgeous dinners here, fabulous parties there, amazing overseas trips with her parents and everything in between. The first time I walked past her in the corridors of Television House, in about 1984, I was in the middle of a *Young Talent Time* rehearsal, so I was wearing something very comfortable but wholly unglamorous. Lori, who looked like she might have been there for a *Vogue* cover shoot, gave me the once over, which meant staring down at the top of my head as I walked past her. I thought to myself: 'She looks like a model; I look really short next to her. I bet she's really stuck-up.'

She was at the studio visiting her friend Joey Perrone, who was one of the other *Young Talent Time* team members, and the guy who later introduced me to my first boyfriend, Gary. On that first encounter, Lori and I didn't give one another the time of day. It was only down the line, when I was dating Gary, that the two of us spoke. Being mutual friends of Joey, Gary and Lori knew one another fairly well, and Gary would always be chirping on about her.

'You have to meet Lori, Dannii. She's so cool, you'll love her. You *have* to meet her.'

I wasn't that bothered, as she'd seemed rather icy to me when we'd crossed paths at Television House, but I agreed to go to lunch with Gary and her. Three hours after taking our seats in the restaurant, the two of us hadn't stopped talking for a single second.

'Here's my number, Dannii,' Lori smiled, as we went our separate ways that afternoon. She handed me a pink silk card, which had her name and number on it embossed in gold. 'Give me a call some time.'

So I did.

I found Lori as fascinating and inspiring a person as she appeared to find me, although she was a year or so older than me and we came from different backgrounds. After that fateful lunch, we started hanging out together regularly, becoming inseparable as each week went by. Eventually, I ended up spending half my life at her parents' place, almost becoming a member of the family. In fact, when Lori's big sister moved out of the family home, her old room became known as Dannii's room, and I got my own key to the front door.

Lori came from quite a wealthy Jewish family. Not having been brought up with any kind of religion, I found the Friday-night Shabbat suppers and the customs the family observed quite intriguing, and, of course, the food was always spectacular. It was an unwritten rule that the whole family had to be there on a Friday evening for Shabbat supper, and to me that was great: everyone talking and catching up on what everyone else in the family was up to over food once a week – what could be better? My favourite meal, though, was the big Sunday brunch that Lori's mum, Ruth, would make, with homemade pumpkin soup, bagels and lox with cream cheese, and chopped herring salad.

When I heard about a job going in my manager Terry Blamey's office, I knew Lori would be perfect for it, and got on the phone to her.

'Terry's looking for someone to help him out,' I told her. 'Things are so full on with Kylie and now it's getting really busy for me, too. Terry needs a right-hand woman, and I think you should go for it.'

'Really?' Lori said. 'I'm not sure, Dan.'

Even after Terry himself had agreed that she would be perfect for the position, Lori wasn't convinced, as she had just started her second year at university, majoring in political science and psychology.

'I guess I could juggle my studies and do it part time,' she finally suggested.

That's what happened, for a while at least. Then Terry needed Lori to travel with me to Japan, and then London, so her academic career eventually went out of the window.

It was February 1991, and Mushroom had licensed my album overseas to various different territories. I'd had three singles out in Australia, and the album, simply called *Dannii*, had sold well. My new European record label, MCA, were confident that it was going to be an absolute smash in the UK, because *Home and Away* was such a huge TV show there and my character, Emma, was so popular. They were also happy that I'd been voted 'Best Female Star' in *TV Hits!* in Britain, and was still on TV every weeknight there, too, because the broadcasts of *Home and Away* in the UK were so far behind Australia. It was the perfect time for me to travel to London – in time for the release of the single 'Love And Kisses'. My best friend, Lori, was coming with me.

When we arrived in London for what was to be a three-week promotional trip, it was wet and freezing cold. Having come from a blistering Aussie summer, it was quite a shock. We'd come via Japan, where I'd been doing radio promotion for the release of 'Love And Kisses', and that had been a shock too – a wonderful culture shock.

Japan was like nowhere else I'd ever been, and everyone we met seemed so very joyous and excited about us being there. The delicacy and politeness of the people was a world away from the boisterous, straight-talking Aussie way I was used to, and nobody spoke English, so we had interpreters everywhere we went. The whole promotional set-up was very efficiently structured. Whenever we had time off, the people at the Japanese record label organised the most amazing sight-seeing trips and nights out for Lori and me. At first, our eager-to-please hosts seemed to take us only to restaurants with Western cuisine, thinking we'd want a steak for dinner every night, but after a couple of days of insisting that we wanted to try real Japanese fare, our wish was granted. My long love affair with Japanese food started on that trip.

We visited the beautiful temples in Kyoto, and a wonderful onsen (a hot spring that you can bathe in) in a small village in the far north of the country. Of course, Lori and I stood out like freaks in a village that wasn't used to Westerners: Lori was a complete 'Glamazon', with her scarlet lips and fabulous clothes, and me standing next to her, much shorter and with long, dyed jet-black hair and bright blue eyes. We found it terribly amusing when a busload of Japanese schoolgirls arrived at one of the temples that Lori and I were being shown around by our interpreter: the giggling teenagers were far more excited about taking pictures of the strange and outlandish Western ladies than the beautiful building they'd come to visit.

London was another experience altogether, and I wasn't quite ready for it when we touched down. Although people had told me many times how popular Aussie TV shows like *Neighbours* and *Home and Away* were in the UK, I wasn't prepared for all the press attention I was about to get.

During the first few weeks, I was sucked into a tornado of television, radio and press interviews, with everyone eager to find out who Dannii was. Kylie was a huge pop star by then, and now here was her little sister . . . While Kylie was seen as the blonde, wholesome pop princess, I seemed to be a mysterious, dark punk version of my older sister: the raven hair, the black leather jacket, the bitchy, tough kid I played on *Home and Away* – it was all there, and that's the way the press were going to play it. This had its advantages at first, to be honest, as it gave me more street cred.

Kylie was often away in Europe or America when I first arrived in London, so Lori and I got to crash at her apartment in Chelsea. It was comfy and central and had pictures of the family all around, so it felt like a little home away from home. Terry would often be away with Kylie, too, so I pretty much had to rely on Lori to organise my life and everything I had to do day-to-day. There was a host of record-company meetings, TV shows and press and radio interviews to coordinate, and Lori did it all – working twenty-five hours a day, eight days a week.

I, meanwhile, felt like I had to be switched on to my 'pop star' setting every time I stepped out of the door, with not a hair out of place and perfect make-up the whole time. This was often a hard enough job in itself and I started to realise what it must have been like when Kylie had first arrived during the frenzy of *Neighbours* publicity. One day, when Lori and I were leaving a TV studio, we got followed down the street by a gaggle of fans who were waving excitedly and screaming at me, 'Emma, Emma!'

'Why are they calling out Emma?' I asked Lori. 'I'm not Emma Jackson any more; I'm Dannii.'

My episodes of *Home and Away* were still showing every teatime in the UK, so as far as they were concerned I was still Emma. I've sometimes thought over the years that Britain's first image of me as cold and tough may have resonated for a lot longer than it should have done.

Pretty soon, my three-week promotional trip was being extended, first to a month and then to three. 'Love And Kisses' had hit the UK Top 10. There was no point in me going back home to Australia, as the second single, 'Success', was hot on its heels. A month after 'Success' charted, and after a bit of remixing and updating under the guidance of my UK A&R manager, Adrian Sykes, my album was released across Europe and Asia. Instead of being called *Dannii*, it was called *Love and Kisses*, like the debut single.

Once Kylie returned from her travels, there wasn't enough room at her place for Lori and me and our huge collection of luggage, so we moved into a hotel in Notting Hill called the Pembridge Court. It was a gorgeous nineteenth-century townhouse near the famous Portobello Road market. Lori and I knew it was the place for us almost as soon as we saw it: each room was lovingly and individually styled and furnished with exquisite antiques, and the place was full of quaint little touches, like framed Victorian gloves and fans. It was divine. It was known as a music-industry favourite, and the staff there couldn't have been more charming. Within weeks, we were on first-name terms with everyone who worked there, and I started to feel right at home. This was fairly fortuitous, as it turned out, because I would live there for the next two years.

Back then, when a record started to climb the charts in the UK, every new artist's dream was to perform on *Top of the Pops*. Coming from Australia, I didn't, at the time, realise the cachet this show had and I knew very little about its long history. Now, having appeared on it so many times over the years, I feel very privileged to have been a part of this British institution while it was still on the air.

There was such a buzz around the show back then, the whole day was an adventure. We normally had to arrive at the BBC first thing in the morning for stuff like camera rehearsals and interviews with *Top of the Pops* magazine. After that, Lori would help me to choose clothes and get my hair and make-up done, so I'd be ready for the noisy and exuberant audience to arrive in the early evening.

When I first went on the show I didn't recognise the importance of it, and consequently wasn't that nervous – after all, I was just singing and dancing on another live TV show, something I'd done all my life. When my single 'Love And Kisses' jumped from number thirty-three in the Top 40 to number fifteen after my debut appearance, I began to realise just how important a spot on *Top of the Pops* could be for an artist – even if said artist was dressed in a silver bra and leather cap.

Yes, once again and this time in Europe, I was becoming known as the girl in the outrageous outfits. I intended to live up to the title with a never-ending parade of crazy gear that I snatched off the rack myself when the stylist wasn't around, and, I reckon, would probably have given Lady Gaga a run for her money. Of course, not all of it was loved or applauded, and I did end up on some of the 'What on earth was she thinking?' pages of various publications.

By the time my single 'Baby Love' was released in the autumn of 1991, I'd had four singles out in less than seven months and was a regular on the iconic *Top of the Pops*. After two months in the Top 40, my album went gold.

I was living out my young girl's dream of being a pop star. *Smash Hits* magazine had voted me Best New Artist of 1991. It was almost impossible to pick up any of the teen publications without finding a 'Dannii' interview or feature inside. Are you scared of spiders, Dannii? What do you think of your sister's new haircut, Dannii? Dannii, do you like English fish and chips? I was suddenly the girl people wanted to know all about, but there was something missing . . .

Although I loved my job, and had Lori with me through all my London adventures, I started to feel something that I'd never really felt before: loneliness. The novelty of living in a hotel, however cosy and friendly it was, was starting to wear thin. With poor Lori stuck in her room surrounded by a mountain of faxes and phones, I began to feel slightly empty whenever I didn't have something to occupy me. The other thing about living at the Pembridge Court was that if we had to go away for more than two or three days at a time on a promotional trip, the record company would insist that we pack up our suitcases, check out of the hotel and then check back in when we came back and start all over again, sometimes in a different room.

I started to miss the simple stuff, like being able to brew my own coffee and make my own meals, and all the fundamental things you do when you have a home of your own. The furniture wasn't my furniture, the walls weren't my walls, and I gave up adorning the hotel rooms with the framed family pictures I'd brought with me from home because I was fed up with packing and unpacking them every time we had to check out. I desperately missed having a group of friends I could hang out with and talk to about something other than whether I liked fish and chips or not. Even having Kylie close at hand in Chelsea wasn't a big help, as we were both always so busy; the chances of us having the same day off were almost zero.

I tried telling myself that I was being ungrateful, that I should be on top of the world. After all, according to *Smash Hits*, I was very nearly the world's sexiest female – second only to Madonna – so I had lots to be thankful for, right? Shouldn't I be happy? Maybe.

But what had started as a fun, three-week promotional trip had morphed into what seemed like an eternity. I was losing touch with all the people I loved back home, and it scared me.

When Lori and I let off steam, though, we'd really let off steam. We'd go to the fabulous Kinky Gerlinky parties in London, and dance the night away with fabulous freaks and glamorous drag queens. Lori would spur me on to have fun and be a little wild.

We were obsessed with buying wigs at that time, and our collection was growing fast. I'd often throw one on to go out clubbing, so I could enjoy myself incognito, without worrying about getting photographed doing something outrageous. When we were out of the country, we'd take our wig-wearing fetish a stage further and have some fun. Whenever we had to do promotion in Europe, we'd pack all the wigs we'd bought in Hyper Hyper, which was a super-trendy mall in London's Kensington High Street, and head for the airport.

I can remember us both once wearing PVC hot pants with matching thigh boots, while hanging out at a very cool club called La Bandouche in Paris. Lori was in a poker-straight black bob wig and false eyelashes, and I was wearing a long red wig that was something like Farrah Fawcett, *circa Charlie's Angels* 1977. We had a blast during those trips, and I'd let loose and feel utterly free. Those were the times I was happy and could banish all the loneliness I'd felt while staring at the four walls in my hotel room. Lori never once asked me if I was scared of spiders or whether or not I liked fish and chips. Thank God for Lori Lipkies!

Chapter 9

Cristal by the Bucketload

One of the most unforgettable trips Lori and I took was in November 1991, when Mushroom Records licensed my album to a small record company in New York. My first release there was a cover of the Stacy Lattisaw disco hit 'Jump To The Beat', which had already been a top-ten single for me in Britain. To mark the occasion of its release in the US, a grand reception was being thrown in my honour. I was very excited to be going back to America to launch the single, particularly as the small label I was signed to had lined up some club gigs for me after the Christmas holidays. As much as I loved London, this trip would be a much needed change and might well blow away a few cobwebs.

Once we were in New York, everything seemed so exciting. The party that the label laid on was a blast and the bubbly flowed like waterfalls. One of the invited guests was none other than Mike Tyson, then at the height of his boxing career. I remember that he spoke very quietly, almost in a whisper, but also that his giant hands almost crushed mine when he greeted me with a rather firm handshake. There were lots of cool people there, and I was very impressed when I met the production team C+C Music Factory, who were absolutely huge at the time.

As Lori and I were taken round and introduced to some of the many 'old school' music-biz types that seemed be on the small label's pay-roll, Lori recognised a couple of the names from a book she'd been reading called *Hit Men*, which was about corruption in the music industry and the old 'payola' system in America, whereby record companies would illegally make under-the-table payments to radio stations so that the stations would play their records – something that had been rife in the fifties and sixties. Lori had quite a giggle about the fact that there were so many of these old timers working for such a small set-up. Some of these guys had apparently been real high-flyers in the music industry twenty or thirty years before, but now here they all were with various jobs in this tiny, family-owned record label. The record-company offices, however, were very ostentatious, with gold ashtrays and marble all over the place, so we thought, 'Great! They must have had a ton of money to throw at us for promotion.' That didn't turn out to be the case at all.

In February 1992, as we made our way across America on an extensive radio and club promotion tour – mostly on buses and trains – the organisation and, indeed, the conditions seemed to get worse and worse. We were left to our own devices most of the time, even though there was a little old guy with a bad attitude who billed himself as 'tour manager' tagging along. Lori and I would constantly be frustrated when he'd disappear at a moment's notice, leaving us to try to figure out what the hell we were supposed to be doing next. Indeed, each hotel we stayed in was worse than the last. Of course, in small towns we didn't expect to be staying at the Four Seasons, but we couldn't understand why we were being put up in such grizzly places when the record company seemed to have so much money. We'd already been told the clubs would not be paying us a fee for playing: any shows we did should be seen as promotion for my record and I should be grateful.

'It's what Madonna did,' the label manager told us. 'It's what everyone does here with pop dance music. You come up through the clubs and let the cool kids discover you.'

Of course, we didn't know any better, and just got on with it, trying at all costs to remain professional. Every morning, Lori would get up to call our 'tour manager' to find out which radio station we were scheduled to be at in which town, or what time the sound check was for the evening's club date, but he couldn't have cared less. There was never an itinerary, and no rehearsals and little advertising for the shows I was playing – and usually no sound check either. In fact, a lot of the time the gigs were me with a backing track at the town disco. Although the record company did organise a couple of 'showcase' gigs on the tour – where people from the music industry were invited to come and see me perform songs from my album – I had to face the fact that I was essentially doing a karaoke tour of the Midwest.

After one gig in Chicago, halfway through the tour, I came off stage and Lori grabbed me and pulled me into the grim, microscopic dressing room. 'There's something not kosher here,' she said to me, with an anxious frown. 'I've just seen the club owner giving our so-called tour manager a big fucking lump of cash. We may not be getting paid for all the work we're doing, Dannii, but somebody sure as hell is.'

'I think we should call Terry,' I said, solemnly.

Lori and I were both still so young and inexperienced. We weren't used to having to deal with this kind of thing and we were completely on our own.

'You're right. I'll do it now,' Lori agreed.

Terry told Lori that this had to be an 'on-the-road' decision, and she'd have to trust her own instincts. After all, he was thousands of miles away. Although he could deal with the record company in New York by phone, only we could decide whether it was worth carrying on with the scheduled promo.

'If Dannii wants to pull the plug on it, then do it,' he said.

Against my better judgement, I decided to carry on.

When we returned to New York for some radio and club promotion there, I hoped things might be better. After all, this was the Big Apple and the clubs were all fabulous. At least the record company might wine and dine us a little after our gruelling schlep across the country. However, when we arrived back in the city – on the train, of course –

nobody was there to meet us, except our less than friendly tour manager, who just handed us the address of the hotel that had been
booked for us.

'It's over that way,' he said to Lori with a vague hand gesture before
he jumped in a cab and went home.

When we finally found the hotel, our hearts sank. We would gladly
have traded it for the very worst of the dumps we'd stayed in on the
road.

'This is the bloody Roach Motel, doll!' Lori said.

I nodded. It really was.

Once inside my room, nauseous from the musty smell, I surveyed
the grubby, worn curtains, tatty wooden furniture and smoke-stained
wallpaper – it was a miserable landscape. 'No,' I said to myself. 'Fuck
this! I may be an unknown artist trying to crack America, but that's no
reason for me to be staying in a room I wouldn't let a donkey sleep in.'
I grabbed the phone and called Lori's room, which was on the floor
below. After quite a few rings, she finally answered, but her voice
sounded far away.

'Hello?'

'It's Dannii. Are you OK? You sound funny.'

'Yes, I'm fine, but I was too scared to touch the phone because it's
so filthy, and I'm certainly not putting it anywhere near my mouth.'

'Gotcha!'

'Are you OK, Dannii? Do you want something?'

'No. Just get me out of here.'

And she did. Right then and there Lori called Gary Ashley, my A&R
man from Mushroom Records, who was in Chicago at the time.

'Gary, we've done the whole tour in shit conditions, but this is the
worst – it's positively infested. We've had it.'

Mercifully, Gary spoke to someone at the label who very quickly
found us somewhere much nicer to stay. Once we'd freshened up, we
headed out to dinner with the head of the record label and some of his
associates at a very swanky bar/restaurant downtown, feeling quite a
lot brighter. As was the norm at any of these dinners, there were at least
forty people coming and going, dining and drinking champagne, all at

the expense of a record label who hadn't booked us on planes from one city to another or put us in half-decent hotels. It wasn't cheap fizz everyone was quaffing either – it was Cristal.

This went on night after night while we were in New York. Lori and I couldn't work out what on earth the deal was with these people: the large flashy dinners with expensive champagne, the opulent offices, the dozens of so-called 'employees' who didn't ever seem to do anything and, best of all, my hard-earned club performance fees going straight into the pocket of that miserable human being who called himself a tour manager.

'It's gotta be a scam,' Lori whispered to me on our last night there.

I had no idea, but by now I just wanted to get back to London and the comfort of the Pembridge Court. Later that night, a few of us were at Nell's club on 14th Street, and still nobody was sipping water. It was Cristal and Cristal and Cristal and then more Cristal. It was Cristal by the bucketload, in fact. There weren't that many of us as it was late: the owner of the label and his main sidekick, and a couple of other people, including the then hotshot record producer Al B. Sure! Lori decided in her wisdom, and possibly slightly inebriated state, that perhaps, as it was our last night, we should order and pay for at least one bottle of champers as we hadn't paid for a single drink all week.

'It's the polite, sophisticated thing to do,' she said with an air of self-assurance.

'Absolutely,' I agreed.

After all, the owner of the label had always been very kind and gen-erous to us personally, despite our misgivings about the label's strange set-up, and the appalling way my so-called tour had been run.

While the others were all dancing, Lori called the waitress over.

'Another bottle of the same,' she said.

Presently, the smiling waitress brought over the open bottle in a silver ice bucket, and handed Lori the check.

'It's totally cool, doll,' Lori said, turning to me while grabbing the bill from the waitress, 'I've got six hundred in cash to cover it, so . . . Oh!'

'What?'

Lori's face was ashen.

'Er . . . that bottle was thirteen hundred and fifty dollars.'

That capped the trip off nicely.

'But there have been forty or fifty people out with us every night, all drinking the stuff non-stop,' Lori said, disbelieving, in the taxi as we headed back to our hotel with seriously damaged credit cards.

'Where the hell does all the money come from?'

'I dunno!' I said.

The next day we returned to the UK none the wiser.

Chapter 10

Brand-New Things

Throughout 1991, I travelled so much I'd started to forget what it was like to have a home or family life. I'd travelled to New Zealand for a while in June to film an independent Aussie movie called *Secrets*, in which I played an introverted Beatles fanatic called Didi. I also went across Southeast Asia to promote the *Love and Kisses* album, and got to see some wonderfully exotic places: Indonesia, Taipei and the Philippines to name a few, but there never seemed to be much opportunity to get back home to see my family in Australia.

London was my main base. Though my manager, Terry Blamey, was now there most of the time, and I still had Lori with me, I felt desperately lonely. All too often, while lying in my pretty four-poster bed at the Pembridge Court Hotel, I'd cry myself to sleep.

Apart from not having made any real friends in London, I wasn't dating either. What was wrong with me? It wasn't like I was a shrinking violet, and I certainly met enough people through work – though I'm not sure how many of the dancers and drag queens Lori and I partied with at Kinky Gerlinky would have fitted the bill. But really! Wasn't I 'Woman of the Year' as far as *Number One* magazine was concerned?

The world's best female pop star according to *Big* magazine? *And*, lest we forget, the world's sexiest female after Madge? Still, dates were very rare, and though I didn't have an awful lot of spare time, a little bit of romance certainly wouldn't have gone amiss.

After one kind thought from someone at my record label, though, things suddenly seemed a little brighter. Penny Feuer was my press officer at MCA Records, and I spent quite a lot of time with her at magazine interviews and photo shoots. I guess she must have sensed that I was having a bit of a hard time. When the managing director of MCA, Tony Powell, threw a lunchtime cocktail party for all the staff and recording artists on the label, Penny suggested I mingle a bit and try to get to know some of my musical stablemates. I remember meeting Kim Wilde, and Wendy James from the band Transvision Vamp, but then Penny ushered me over to meet an artist named Terry Ronald, who was laughing and chatting with my A&R manager, Adrian Sykes.

'Terry's big in Spain,' Penny said with a wry smile and a wink.

Terry laughed and threw back a comically evil stare. 'Bitch!' he said.

Penny was also Terry's press officer at the label and the two of them had become good friends. He was older than me – in his mid-twenties – but he was confident and a lot friendlier than some of the other people I'd been introduced to.

'I know exactly who you are,' he said, and we shook hands.

It was a few weeks later, in late September 1991, when Terry Ronald and I met again. I had to fly out to Spain on a promotional trip, and I was disappointed because Lori was in America and was unable to come with me. I'd been invited to a swanky music-business awards dinner on my last night there. As I walked into the plush lobby of the gorgeous hotel in Madrid with some of my European promotional team, I was happy to see a familiar face coming towards me.

'Hey, remember me?' Terry said, smiling. 'Well, I've just been forcibly ejected from the fucking hotel bar for wearing shorts. Literally snatched my martini out of my hand and marched me out. I said to them, "Are you insane? These shorts are linen from Paul Smith, and